THE
POWER RESET

A BOLD GUIDE TO RECLAIMING EMOTIONAL
FREEDOM, CLARITY, AND CONFIDENCE

CASSIE SOBELTON

Copyright © 2025 Cassie Sobelton

All rights reserved.

No part of this publication may be reproduced, distributed, or transmitted in any form or by any means, including photocopying, recording, or other electronic or mechanical methods, without the prior written permission of the publisher, except as permitted by U.S. copyright law.

Paperback ISBN: 978-1-950043-65-1

A QUICK NOTE

This book is a guide, but the real work starts with you.

As you read, pause when something resonates.

Mark what stirs something in you.

Try the tools. Trust your pace.

For bonus resources, meditations, and next steps, visit:

CassieSobelton.com.

You'll find everything you need to stay supported and anchored as you reclaim your voice, strength, and power.

DEDICATION

For Rob: My love, my partner, and my best friend.

I love you beyond words.

In every season, in every chapter, you have shown up with unwavering presence. You support my dreams, celebrate my strengths, and remind me of who I am when I forget. You've never asked me to shrink. You've only ever made space for me to shine.

Through my hardest moments—when I literally could not stand, when I could barely move—you carried the weight of our world without complaint. You turned care into a daily ritual of kindness. And somehow, even amidst the chaos, you still left your morning notes of love and praise. Each one with a quiet reminder: You are not alone. You are cherished.

You've taught me the power of relaxation, that there is joy in the simple things, steadfast loyalty, soul-deep partnership, and what it means to be truly met in love. Thank you for walking beside me on our spiritual journey, for growing with me, for loving me, and for believing in me without hesitation.

This book wouldn't exist without your heart behind it.

And neither would I—at least not like this.

CONTENTS

Introduction 1

Chapter 1
Empowered Spirituality 7

Chapter 2
Transforming Pain into Power 15

Chapter 3
The Language of Your Emotions 21

Chapter 4
Instinct as a Sacred Guide 31

Chapter 5
Boundaries Without Bitterness 40

Chapter 6
Truth Without Illusion: Seeing Others Clearly 48

Chapter 7
Intuition Speaks: Will You Listen? 56

Chapter 8
Your Body Never Lies 64

Chapter 9
Reclaiming the Power of Your Body: Biology in Balance 76

Chapter 10
Reclaiming the Power of Your Mind: From Shadow to Strength 87

Conclusion
Owning Your Power and Purpose 100

About the Author 108

Connect With Me 109

INTRODUCTION

Speaking your truth isn't always easy. It requires, first, the realization of your truth. It requires breaking through the noise of society, your family, your community, and marketing and advertising. It requires thinking outside the box. It requires deep examination of complex topics. It requires honesty with yourself and others about what you truly believe. It requires a bold authenticity that many, especially women, are taught to silence at a very young age.

Many of us were taught to value politeness over honesty, political correctness over justice, reputation over righteousness, conformation over rebellion. We were silenced as children when we disagreed with adults or societal truths. We were often told what to believe rather than being allowed to formulate our own conclusions, based on our own thought process, research, education, and experience. It's far easier to control children who blindly accept what we tell them than those taught to navigate their own truths. And this has led to a society of people who have learned to be polite and accept truths handed to them rather than swim against the tide to seek our own.

Living in this manner has stripped so many of their power. The power we are inherently born with that eventually we tuck away, in the name of politeness. The power we so often give away to political and spiritual leaders, religious institutions, gurus, medical professionals, the government, and various other individuals in our lives.

Have you ever seen a child shamed by an adult for not giving a hug or a kiss to someone they didn't want to? Maybe they were forced to hug Uncle James, in the name of politeness, rather than be allowed to make their own decision on how they greet this relative. It's a very small example of how we are programmed at a young age that politeness, and making our elders happy, trumps personal boundaries.

I'm not saying that children should rule the roost. I'm not saying that a child should not be taught to be polite and social. I am saying that teaching that child the many ways she can acknowledge Uncle James and allowing her to choose which she feels most comfortable with is teaching her how to be powerful. It teaches this child that her body is hers and she can behave in the way that feels most comfortable to her. She can greet Uncle James with a handshake, a high five, a hug or kiss, as it feels appropriate.

Taking it a step further, could they be taught to communicate their boundaries more effectively and without guilt? Could young women or men be taught to express their discomfort when they are treated in ways that do not feel good to them? When they are touched in ways they do not appreciate, talked to in ways that are not appropriate, or discriminated against for being of a particular gender?

In our society, girls have to deal with the expectation to be polite even more than boys. Girls are taught to be sweet and kind. Boys are taught to be tough and not show emotions. Both ways are flawed. It has gotten a little better over the years, but this way of teaching children still persists in many parts of the country. We are stripping girls of their power and teaching boys to put a false front up to cover theirs. The truth of our feelings should not be silenced or hidden. They are the source of our true power—when we learn how to harness and express them properly.

There are many examples of ways we give up our power. Consider how many people override their intuition when a physician tells them their labs are fine after expressing concern about something. So many people take their word as gospel instead of pushing for more tests or going for a second opinion because they assume their white coat gives them more knowledge than the person's own lived experience.

Or how about when a boss asks you to do something you don't feel comfortable with? You know it isn't a wise move, but you agree, just to avoid conflict.

Have you ever over-committed yourself, believing you were being kind? You said "yes" when you meant "no," abandoning yourself, your desires and your needs, all for the approval of others.

These are all common ways we give away our power in today's world. Most of these patterns are inherited, culturally reinforced, and rooted in fear, habit, or misunderstood ideas about what is "right" and "wrong."

Of course, these patterns are further reinforced by the roles we play in society.

I want to tell you a story about gender in American society. In my first year of college, like many, I took all 100-level lecture classes. This typically meant hundreds of students in a large lecture hall, with a single professor. I interacted in class as I thought normal—I completed my assignments, I was decently familiar with what was going on in class, and I had met all my instructors, of course. By the end of the semester, four out of five of my professors asked the same question of me: "Did you go to an all-girls school growing up?"

I was surprised when the first professor asked because, yes, I had gone to an all-girls high school. The second time made me raise an eyebrow. How odd that two of my professors asked that. The third asking was downright weird. And when the fourth asked, I was shocked and said, "How do you know that?!"

That fourth professor said something I will never forget. He said, "You speak up in class, you introduced yourself to me, and you have no issues challenging authority or your male counterparts in class. That is rare behavior for a young woman, and the only time we see it is following all-girls schooling."

It turns out that girls take a backseat to boys in co-ed schools. Boys are just naturally louder and more dominant, and simply because of their presence, girls do not learn to have the same voice in class. The same can be said for women in business, society, and probably many other areas of their life. Of course, there are exceptions, but that conversation with my professor made me highly value my all-girls high school experience.

The good news is that our power is never truly stripped from us. It is temporarily caged, waiting to be released again. You have the ability, the strength, the courage, and if you are reading this book, the drive and desire, to take your power back.

We've spent a lot of time talking about power—losing it and taking it back—but what is power exactly? Some might associate it negatively with corruption, control over others, or greed. Others may think of it more positively as it relates to financial freedom or strong control over one's life.

For the purposes of this book, I ask you to consider power as it relates to you individually: power over yourself, your emotions, your thoughts, your body, your beliefs, your experiences, your needs, your desires, your truth, your personal rights. Power over others is not true power. Only the weak need to control others. True power is owning your own strength and allowing everyone else to own theirs. A powerful person only wants to lift others up; to assist them in finding their own power.

Powerlessness is a debilitating experience. I use the word "experience" and not "feeling" because being without power is much more than a feeling. It's to be without strength or ability, wholly unable to act and influence. It's a state of helplessness.

If you experience powerlessness in any part of your life, you can change that. You can retrain your brain; you can become the CEO of your life. Powerlessness is not an identity. It's possible to come back from a place of powerlessness. You can take your power back.

Many find it easier to own their power when supported by others. The #MeToo movement of 2017 is a powerful example of this. Women—who had previously been silenced—came out in droves with their personal stories of sexual assault and harassment. This movement spread like wildfire, demonstrating the extreme misogynistic behavior that had been prevalent and accepted in our society.

The sheer number of social media posts, articles, news segments, and media spots that ensued showed how many people (mostly women) felt powerful enough to share their story—sometimes for the first time in their lives.

But why did it take a movement for these women to speak up? Was misogyny so engrained in our society that speaking up seemed useless? Did so many of these women truly believe they deserved this type of treatment? Were these women fearful for their jobs, their families, or even their lives?

Possibly they were taught at a young age that their bodies were not totally theirs.

Many of the issues women experience happen because we haven't learned how to effectively communicate our boundaries. We are afraid to speak our truths because we were taught to be polite. But politeness and powerlessness are not one and the same. They have often been associated, but there is always a way to be polite *and* powerful. It just takes a specific type of training and mindset.

Standing up for oneself takes tremendous skill. The above example is about female empowerment, but so many segments of society are discriminated against, and the same is true for them. We must first educate ourselves on how to hold and effectively communicate our boundaries within the framework of our society. This goes for all races, genders, sexual preferences, ages, religious affiliations, and disabilities.

The idea of being the CEO of one's life is an interesting concept that can help you own your power. Consider a business. The CEO is responsible for the business's successes and failures. There is no skirting whose responsibility it is. Even if tough things happened and blows were dealt, we expect the CEO to manage those situations and steer the company into green pastures. The same is true for your life.

No matter what cards you were dealt to start, or what happens along the way, you are the CEO of your life. No one is coming to save you. It is

100% your responsibility to own your situation. Your past, your current situation, and your future life are completely your responsibility.

You were never meant to live at half power. But somewhere along the way, life taught you to second-guess your instincts, abandon your needs, and stay small to keep the peace. This book is a call back to your full self. Through grounded insights, emotional intelligence tools, and mind-body-spirit practices, it will help you strip away the noise of outside expectations so you can finally hear your own voice again and, most importantly, trust it fully.

In these pages, you'll explore how to reclaim your boundaries with compassion, pursue your desires without guilt, and stop giving your power away to experts, systems, or inherited beliefs. You'll learn how stress manifests in the body, how trauma can become growth, and how you can use intuitive tools, from body-based wisdom to emotional attunement, to realign with your truth. This isn't about becoming somebody new. This is about remembering who you were before the world taught you to doubt it.

This book invites you to stop performing, start listening, and step into the kind of strength that doesn't need to shout, because it's rooted, real, and truly yours.

Life will always toss curveballs, emergencies, heartbreak, chaos, drama, people who trigger us, and systems that disappoint. That part isn't going away. But this book will teach you how to stay rooted in your power so you don't get knocked over by every storm. You'll learn how to stand firm, not because life got easier but because you got anchored. You will learn how to respond instead of react, how to hold your boundaries without shutting down, and how to protect your peace without losing connection.

True power isn't about controlling life. It's about expanding your capacity to meet it with clarity, resilience, and grace.

CHAPTER 1

Empowered Spirituality

I grew up in a Catholic family. I spent a lot of time with my devout Catholic grandfather, who went to seminary and was nearly a priest before meeting my grandmother. He was a good man, strictly religious. Even at a young age, I remember debating religious topics with him and questioning the rules of Catholicism and the existence of hell.

That time with him and my attendance at Catholic school gave me ample time to debate spirituality and religion as a child. Paradoxically, I was pushed away from the church by this schooling, and without even knowing it, I developed a deep sense of personal spirituality that would later emerge as a powerful force in my life. Much of this can be attributed to my Catholic high school, ironically. For the first time in my Catholic schooling, the religious curriculum in my all-girls high school was not 100% Christian based. They allowed us to explore multiple faiths and spiritual ideas. I took classes on Buddhism, Judaism, spirituality, even a class called Death and Dying, which helped us explore the idea of what lies beyond death and how to handle the dying on this physical plane.

Here's the thing, I find many aspects of religion fascinating and fantastic. Religion can be deeply meaningful and supportive, especially when practiced with openness and intention. Religion can provide a strong sense of community and belonging, be a moral and ethical compass, provide spiritual connection, offer ritual, tradition, hope and resilience. Many religions encourage acts of charity, social justice, and care for others. When rooted in love, religion can be a powerful vessel for healing, growth, and soul-filled living.

While religion is often presented as a source of peace, morality, and meaning, history tells a far more complicated story. Wars have been fought, lives lost, and entire populations oppressed in the name of God because humans stepped between God and the individual.

From crusades to colonization, from witch trials to modern-day extremism, religion has been weaponized to justify violence, control, and discrimination. While many dismiss these atrocities as the work of fanatics, the truth is more uncomfortable: the structures, hierarchies, and fear-based doctrines within many religions have made these abuses possible.

Beyond the global scale, damage has also occurred quietly. Damage within families, communities, and to individuals occurs when religion teaches people to mistrust their instincts, suppress their desires, and give away their power in the name of being "good" or "worthy."

It's such a slippery slope and while there are many wonderful, empowering parts of most religions, they frequently teach us to give away our power.

Many religions teach us to place authority outside of the self—in a leader, scripture, church, or institution. This can condition people to distrust their inner voice and look externally for validation, permission, or redemption.

Religions often use fear of punishment to regulate behavior rather than fostering self-awareness or emotional intelligence. This can create reactive obedience rooted in fear instead of conscious, empowered thinking.

Some religions label desire, sexuality, curiosity, or questioning as sinful. People feel ashamed of their natural instincts and expressions, teaching them to ignore the signals of their body or deny their truths.

Religions often value dogma more than personal connection to the divine. Rather than being guided into their own personal spiritual experiences, people are told what to believe and how to access that spirituality.

Some religions disempower women and marginalized groups.

Leadership might be male dominated, and feminine wisdom, intuition, or roles are omitted or diminished.

This can be dangerous because it disconnects people from their inner compass, which makes it easier to manipulate them. It creates shame and guilt around natural human experiences, which can lead to repression and internal conflict. It fosters dependency on authority figures, who can exploit emotionally, financially, or sexually. It discourages questioning, which is vital for self-growth and discovery.

Many people have confided in me that they were not given the space to question religion as a child, such as I was. Maybe they were shut down and told to blindly believe. Many do not remember the exact conversations, but the beliefs became engrained. It's just another example of how we teach children to give away power—in this case out of fear.

People who didn't get the opportunity to claim the positive parts of spirituality have missed a critical element of personal empowerment. Spirituality can connect us, give us inner knowing, meaning, love, courage, and truth, without the dogma that so many of us feel, in our gut, is out of alignment with our personal truth or lived experience. If this is you, it is important to know that you can heal from religious trauma or conditioning and build a relationship directly with the sacred.

I strongly believe spiritual connection is empowering and needs to be made daily, before leaving the house, to live a balanced life. I believe when I make this personal connection through prayer, meditation, or spiritual study, I am far less likely to fall into reactive behavior, anger, frustration, or any other emotions and actions that could lower my vibration or hurt myself and others. I believe my connection to my spirituality has saved my life many times. It guides me, empowers me, and sustains me.

Using spirituality to connect to your inner authority is a direct path to personal power. True spirituality connects you to something greater, and doesn't require you to lose any of yourself. It reminds you that you're not alone in this world and helps to provide clarity, comfort, and purpose. You feel empowered when you realize that you are a part of this greater energy, not beneath it.

If you've ever practiced yoga, you've likely heard the phrase "Namaste" at the end of class. Namaste is a Sanskrit word that roughly translates to "I bow to you." This is often accompanied by a bow of the head, or even the body, showing respect or even worship. The meaning here is the acknowledgement that each of us has a piece of God inside of us; we bow to that piece of the Creator inside every human walking the earth. We are in essence a piece of the whole, and the power is not outside of us but within us.

Whether you call it the Creator, universe, God, source, life force, or your higher self, building a personal relationship with a power greater than yourself will allow you to download *your* answers for *yourself*. Unlike some religions, which often tell us what to believe, spirituality invites you to listen inward. It teaches you to trust your intuition, your body, and your experiences. This kind of inner attunement becomes a compass for navigating life in a way that cannot be manipulated or taken away. Once you stop outsourcing your decisions and start honoring your truth, you will feel empowered to be the truest you.

A deep sense of spirituality will affirm that you were never broken or unworthy. It helps you unlearn shame-based belief systems and remember that you are inherently whole and sacred. You are guaranteed that simply because you were born. Just being you, no matter what has happened to you in the past or what mistakes you have made, gives you the right to this empowered connection to spirit. This remembering is radical.

You can use spirituality to build emotional resilience. Through practices like meditation, breathwork, prayer, ritual, or being in nature, you can learn to calm your nervous system, restore perspective, and recenter yourself in moments of chaos. This kind of inner grounding allows you to face challenges without falling apart or losing yourself.

Above all else, spiritual growth is about confronting hard truths with courage and developing the tools to own your shadow self and take responsibility for your thoughts and actions. It allows you to keep coming back to your center and aligning with your highest self.

I study many different types of spirituality and religion and have formed my own personal philosophy and spiritual path. Instead of fear or control, these practices fill me with empowerment and fulfillment and allow me to tune into my intuition. A spiritual study that teaches you tools to regulate your nervous system and alchemize your trauma into resilience and healing, and that allows you to move from self-betrayal to self-trust, is life changing.

Listening to your inner guidance through rituals, prayer, meditation, visualization, and synchronicity will help you merge mysticism with personal empowerment. There are a myriad of options to guide you to radical self-acceptance of your life, your challenges, and your purpose and potential here on Earth, including yogic traditions, Kabbalah, energy practices, movement techniques, somatic healing, breathwork, astrology, and earth-based traditions.

Below are some practices, journal prompts, and tools that can help you to align with your spirituality:

- **A meditation to connect to something greater**
  Practice:
  Step 1: Sit in silence and envision the energy of a greater power in front of you (God, source, universe, higher self).
  Step 2: Now see that energy as a mirror reflecting back to you what is inside you.
  Step 3: Breathe deeply and ask, "What within me is already divine?"

  Journal:
  When do I feel most connected to something greater than myself?
  What does it feel like to co-create with that energy, instead of begging for help or waiting to be saved?

- **A practice to heal shame and reclaim worthiness**
  Practice:
  Step 1: Stand in front of a mirror.
  Step 2: Connect with your eyes for as long as possible. (Begin with ten seconds and work up to one minute or more over time.)
  Step 3: Say "I am already enough. I am already whole. I do not need to earn my worth." Say it until you believe it or feel your resistance begin to soften.

  Journal:
  What parts of myself have I judged or rejected because of past teachings?
  If I believed I was already whole, how would I speak to myself differently today?

- **A practice to build emotional resilience through nature**
  Practice:
  Step 1: If possible, go outside and touch nature (bare feet in grass, hand touching a tree, etc.). If you cannot go outside, look out the window.
  Step 2: Take three slow breaths while focusing on beauty in nature.
  Step 3: Focus on how nature co-regulates your nervous system.
  Step 4: Say "I am safe. I am steady. I am grounded. I am supported."

  Journal:
  What does my body need right now to return to center?
  What practices help me feel grounded when life feels chaotic or heavy?

- **A practice to see that everything facilitates growth**
  Practice:
  Step 1: Sit alone and reflect on your past.

Step 2: Ask yourself: "What if nothing was a mistake?"
Step 3: Ask yourself: "What if nothing is a punishment or bad luck?"
Step 4: Ask yourself: "What if the very experience I am trying to outrun or erase is actually the experience that holds the key to my evolution?"

Journal:
Consider a past "mistake" and write a story about it being a signpost from your highest self, directing you to your next spiritual lesson. What did it teach you? Where did it take you? What were some blessings that came out of it that otherwise would not have shown up in your life?
What is something in your life that you felt was bad luck, but you can now see it as sacred redirection?
What is something in your life that is currently a "problem?" What could it be trying to teach you? What evolution does it hold for you?

- **A practice to build accountability and integrity**
  Practice:
  Step 1: At the end of every day, before bed, sit quietly alone and take ten deep breaths.
  Step 2: Ask yourself: "Where did I show up in alignment with my highest self today?"
  Step 3: Ask yourself: "Where did I react from fear, ego, or defensiveness?"
  Step 4: Ask yourself: "What can I shift tomorrow?"
  No judgment – just observe.
  Step 5: Ask for forgiveness from your higher power (whatever you call it).
  Step 6: Listen for the response: "You are forgiven." If you do not hear it, say it to yourself.

Journal:
What truths about myself am I afraid to see but ready to own?
What does it mean to live in integrity, even when no one is watching?
What habits can I begin to change tomorrow to live in more integrity and with greater spiritual purpose?

When you've begun reconnecting with your inner compass, you'll be better equipped to see life itself as a spiritual curriculum. A strong spiritual practice isn't just about feeling calm or centered, it's about learning to trust that every experience, even the painful ones, are here to evolve you. Challenges stop feeling random or cruel when you start seeing them as invitations for growth. The more you practice listening inward, the more you'll realize that life is always speaking to you. Every heartbreak, every delay, every illness, and every obstacle can be a message, if you're willing to listen.

When we begin to see life through this lens, everything changes. Instead of thinking something is happening to you, you can begin seeing that everything is here to teach you. That shift alone is an act of reclaiming power. You are no longer a victim to circumstances but instead a participant in your own transformation.

Pain doesn't disappear, it instead becomes purposeful. Every challenge, every situation becomes crystal clear, and you become so profoundly certain that it is just another part of your phoenix-rising story that setbacks become nothing more than a driver to a higher destiny. And when this certainty fills you, you are unstoppable.

This type of connection is not as hard as you may think it will be to achieve. I did it and I promise you can too.

CHAPTER 2

Transforming Pain into Power

This chapter is about learning to recognize challenges as spiritual assignments and discovering how to turn your pain into power. Not by skipping over or sugarcoating the hard stuff, but by facing it, head on, with the eyes of a seeker and the heart of a warrior. When you see your wounds as initiation, you stop being defined by what happens to you and start becoming who you were always meant to be.

Sometimes life speaks to us through external events. Other times, it whispers, or screams, through the body. Pain isn't just something to numb or avoid; it's a form of communication. Physical symptoms, chronic tension, and emotional heaviness are often signals of deeper imbalances in your life, relationships, or inner world.

When something is out of alignment, your body feels it first. But the empowering part of this is that pain can become a portal, a message, a wake-up call. Pain is here to teach you and when you stop seeing it as the enemy and start seeing it as a guide, you gain the ability to correct the imbalances that caused it in the first place. This will transform your suffering into radical, lasting change.

The truth is most of us are deeply disconnected. Disconnected from our bodies, our emotions, and from our spirit or higher self. We have been raised in a culture that prioritizes productivity over presence, logic over intuition, and outward success over internal alignment. We normalize stress, chronic pain, and emotional burnout. We aren't taught to pause and ask why. We aren't taught to see our symptoms as messages from our soul.

And so those small misalignments (fatigue, tension, indigestion, irritability) go unacknowledged. We are told to toughen up. And the misalignments grow. They scream. The discomfort becomes undeniable.

This disconnection is what causes imbalances to manifest into illness and injury. The body becomes a messenger, and if you don't listen, it gets louder and louder. God turns up the volume. Not as punishment but as an invitation to connect. A redirection from the wrong path.

Instead of answering that invitation, many of us give our power away. We give our power to doctors and authority figures who might not understand us, or worse, don't believe us. We are taught to ignore our gut instincts and obey the experts. But what happens when the expert gets it wrong?

I learned this the hard way.

As a child, I dealt with persistent digestive issues and chronic bloating, symptoms I now know were signs of Crohn's disease. But back then, I accepted the pain as normal. I pushed through it, ignored it, and lived with it. I was young and didn't know how abnormal it was, let alone how to hear the messages of imbalance being sent through the pain.

I also blew out my knee at age ten after a bike accident, leading to my first minor surgery. It was only the beginning of many physical breakdowns I couldn't yet recognize as spiritual teachers.

Here's the thing: when kids are experiencing challenges like this, they can't possibly understand that they are messengers. Without parents or teachers to help children learn this, they are bound to continue these patterns until they're mature enough to seek knowledge that will help them stop the cycle. It's not their fault. But it is a redirection being sent by a higher power. Something must change.

And if nothing changes, the challenges will continue.

The turning point came for me in my early twenties. During a martial arts defense class, I shattered my tibia in a simulated attack. The pain was intense and immediate. I dragged myself to the hospital, only to be turned away by an ER doctor with a misdiagnosis of a "sprain" because I was "not in enough pain to have a broken leg." Apparently that high tolerance for pain I developed as a child was coming back to bite me. I begged for an X-ray but he refused. He sent me home, telling me to ice and rest my leg. I reluctantly followed his orders.

A full week later, still in agonizing pain, I returned to the hospital. The new doctor ordered an X-ray and what it revealed was devastating: my tibia was so badly shattered that a cadaver bone, plates, and screws were necessary to repair my leg. I couldn't walk for ten months. It took a year of physical therapy to regain basic movement. I still have limitations from that injury today. All because I let someone in a white coat silence my intuition.

And I swore I would never do that again.

Shortly thereafter, when I was diagnosed with Crohn's disease, I was told I'd be on over twenty pills a day, for life. I was told more surgeries would ensue, possibly a colostomy bag. But I knew what would happen if I followed orders blindly and ignored the possibility of this being a sign from my higher self. I had lived that story already.

So I took a different path. I thanked the physician for getting me this far and found a new physician who was more holistic-minded and who agreed to monitor me, without further intervention. My family thought I was crazy; my initial physician was stunned. I went back to school, studied holistic nutrition and yoga, and went deep down the path of mind-body-spirit connection. Within a year, I reversed all my symptoms and came off all my medications. I lost close to forty pounds. I left my job and found another more in line with this newfound passion for holistic health and healing. More than twenty-five years later, I am still in remission and working in my dream career.

While it may be the norm in our culture to keep pushing forward in life and career, neglecting the toll on physical and emotional health and well-being, it's not okay. It's important to recognize that it is not strong or courageous to continuously push aside pain, discomfort, addictions, anxiety, and depression in the quest to be successful or get ahead. It's going to catch up with you eventually.

The body is a tool that a higher power or the universe is using to portray something to us, but we must be willing to acknowledge it. Like most Americans, when I was younger, I was ill-equipped to recognize what was going on in my body as a manifestation of imbalances. I was powerless without this information. So instead of dealing with the root of the issue, I continued to deny it, bury it, cover it up, and push it aside.

When I matured into this knowledge and started seeing every trauma as a growth opportunity, my recoveries looked very different. They started being catalysts to major life transformations. From career changes to weight loss, relationship changes to philosophy shifts, very little remained from my "old life" to my "new life."

My most recent challenge came from a bike accident that shattered my elbow and tore the meniscus in both knees. I underwent two major surgeries and faced two years of painful, ongoing recovery. The pain was deeper and more consuming than anything I'd experienced before. This time, I leaned into it. I knew there were a few big lessons in front of me. The larger the pain, the larger the lessons.

Unlike previous surgery recoveries, I did not use opioids. Oddly, only six months before the accident, I had launched a new company called Wellness Collection®. We manufacture multiple lines of products, including CBD products. I reformulated some of those products while recovering and through rehabilitation to be stronger and more effective. I learned so much about holistic pain management that does not involve narcotics.

At first, I relied on THC to cope, but I began to notice my connection to spirit was slipping. I couldn't hear my inner voice. I felt disconnected from my higher self. That awareness woke me up. I saw two distinct, possible futures: one numbed out by substances, the other guided by presence. I chose clarity. I let go of the THC and returned to my spiritual center.

During this same period, my partner, Rob, became my rock. He stepped up in every way: bathing me, feeding me, managing our home, and holding space for me when I was at my lowest. His care was unwavering and filled with love, and it deepened our relationship in the most beautiful way. He taught me what true partnership looks like: grounded, selfless, steady. I'll forever be grateful for the way he showed up when I needed him the most.

And with all this came the financial strain of being unable to work. I had to rethink how I earned money, how I saw money, and how I defined security. I confronted the scarcity stories I'd carried since childhood and began rewriting my relationship with wealth.

Pain was the portal. It forced me to listen, to evolve, to reclaim my voice. It helped me correct multiple imbalances in my life.

And I want you to know—you can do this too.

You don't have to wait for a catastrophe. Start by acknowledging any imbalances you might have today. Listen when your body whispers so it doesn't have to scream. Be willing to explore the messages beneath your symptoms. Ask your pain what it is trying to teach you.

The most important place to begin is by zeroing in on your mind-body-spirit connection as your internal guidance system. It's what helps you make aligned choices. It's how you build a relationship with your body, your emotions, and your soul. When this connection is strong, you don't need to outsource your power. You become your own authority.

So, what does that look like in practice?

It looks like listening when your body speaks. Honoring your intuition, even when others disagree. Pausing to reflect before you react. Making food, movement, and lifestyle choices that support your energy. Creating space for stillness. Tracking patterns. Making empowered decisions rooted in self-awareness.

Here are a few tools that will support you on that journey:

- **Journal Prompt:** What physical symptoms or recurring issues have I ignored or minimized over the years? Are there any chronic symptoms? When is the first time I remember them

showing up and what was happening in my life at that time? What might these symptoms be trying to show me?
- **Meditation:** Lay down on your back. Put one hand over your heart and one hand over your belly. Slow your breathing and breathe deeply. Ask your body "What do you need me to know?" Let the answer arise.
- **Activity:** Keep a body journal for one week. Each day, track any physical sensations or pain and what was happening emotionally or mentally at that time.
- **Journal Prompt:** Write a letter to your body, apologizing for all the times you didn't listen. Then write a reply from your body back to you. What wisdom does your body want to share?
- **Visualization:** Imagine a glowing light moving through your body, illuminating any areas of pain, tension, or discomfort. Ask those areas what they need. Offer gratitude for them communicating with you. Envision healing flowing into those areas.
- **Integration Practice:** Before bed, do a three-minute scan of your day. Ask: Where did I feel most disconnected? When did I override my needs? How can I better support myself tomorrow?

Pick one of these activities to try today. Then add another in every few days or weekly to slowly start integrating this practice.

You are already powerful. Pain is not your punishment; it is your teacher. Your transformation begins when you stop resisting and start listening. Healing isn't about fixing something broken. It's about returning to the wholeness that is already inside of you.

And once you've reclaimed your physical and spiritual alignment, it's time to meet the next messenger: your emotions. Because if the body is your compass, your emotions are its voice. And learning to understand that language is how you begin to master your inner world.

CHAPTER 3

The Language of Your Emotions

Emotional intelligence, being able to identify and understand your emotions, is a crucial skill. But many people are completely out of touch with their feelings, and even identifying them seems like an overwhelming task, much less processing them. Instead, we numb out with distractions such as work, television, social media, children, and various activities. The many distractions leave us out of touch and unable to compute the messages the body is trying to send.

I recently had a conversation with a friend about a new law in our city allowing people to beg for money on the streets. Many citizens are saying they are angry that these "beggars" are allowed to sit on the corner and beg in such a way. My friend said that the people should have to go get jobs, and he was angry about it.

Because I'm all about identifying TRUE emotions, not secondary feelings, I had to dig a little deeper with my friend and ask, "Are you really angry about this, or are you maybe uncomfortable? These are very different emotions." We then talked about whether guilt is playing a role in this situation, which was possibly leading to discomfort and ultimately anger. Did he have any compassion for these people? Did he feel like they were trying to take advantage of him or "the system" (that he funds with his tax dollars)? We discussed how all these emotions could be getting lumped together and creating a stronger emotional response than he intended.

People who are not attuned to themselves can let their feelings turn to anger rather than realizing how many factors are at play and allowing compassion or other positive emotions to also surface. We see this all around us, don't we? This type of emotional confusion shows up in the media, especially in politics, every day. Anger is an easier emotion to bring up than compassion. People feel powerless to make changes in our world and in our government, so they become angry and vengeful. The real emotion here isn't true anger—rather it is powerlessness that manifests as anger.

The inability to identify feelings is an epidemic in our society. People are out of tune with body, mind, and spirit, and because of this are unable to do the inward work necessary to process feelings. The good news is you can take the steps to learn how to get attuned—and this is very empowering.

Often, I will encourage people to begin by learning stress reduction techniques. This way, they can reduce their stress and fear. Next, they can start to identify what they are truly feeling, beneath the pressure of their fight-or-flight response. A state of stress can lead to emotional blindness, so we first must calm that.

Sometimes this process is so uncomfortable that people would prefer to stay busy, overstressed, and distracted than face their emotions. Examples of this include sitting alone at a restaurant or even simply at a red light while driving and feeling compelled to pull out a phone to check social media, or being unable to eat a meal at home without having the television on.

We have been so conditioned as a society to be continually stimulated that most people can't (or won't) be alone with themselves and their thoughts and feelings without distraction. I'm not saying that entertainment, iPhones, tablets, or even books are bad, but if we are using them as a distraction from our emotions, this can be a roadblock to healing and empowerment. We are seeing this more and more with children these days. They are becoming addicted to electronic distractions.

Even without the electronics we have today, many of us were taught as children to "get over it" or "be quiet" instead of learning to process feelings. How many times have you heard a parent in a grocery store shut down a child who is experiencing a strong emotion? How many times did you experience this in your own childhood? The majority of people—including parents and teachers—aren't equipped to teach children how to process their emotions because they don't even know how to do it themselves.

Instead, we learn early in life to stuff emotions or cover them up with a different emotion that seems safer and more acceptable. These covered, hidden, and stuffed emotions will always bubble up, though. Whether they manifest in an explosion of anger or violence, an addiction, or health problems, emotions always make themselves known. There's really no avoiding them.

Some time ago, I was at a seminar and a woman was talking about having to deal with an irrational husband who tends to fly off the handle and freak out on the regular. She shared that it was hard to keep her composure and not lash out at him too. It brought up an important question. Is it possible to keep your emotional maturity even if someone is being awful to you? If someone calls you a name, do you automatically react in anger? Do you even consider that this person might be correct and, while he may not be delivering the lesson in an appropriate manner, he is delivering a message you should consider?

There is a certain amount of mirroring that goes on in relationships. This begs the question: What are people mirroring back to you? And what does this say about your own emotions? Remember too that if you are around people who are angry all of the time, it becomes easy to be angry too.

One thing to remember when you have people in your life who are angry or extremely difficult is that they are likely emotionally stunted. We all are to a certain extent, but some have evolved further than others in their adult lives. I have found it is helpful to step back and see the difficult person for where she is emotionally—even as she is lashing out in anger. I look at this person like I would look at a five-year-old child if she was having a temper tantrum, because that's basically what is happening. There is something inside this person that hasn't evolved emotionally, so she begins acting like a child.

My response is to stop and ask myself what I would say to a child I loved. Would I return her tantrum-throwing with screaming and yelling? No, of course not. Instead, I would say, "I think you are overreacting right now…I love you very much, but the things you are saying are hurtful. So let's take some time to step back, and we will talk about this later when you aren't feeling so upset."

I would also consider what this person is saying. While she is possibly overreacting, there is most likely some truth to the underlying topic. People are nothing but messengers, delivering powerful insights. If you can learn to see beyond their emotionally immature traits (like anger), you could find nuggets of wisdom for self-growth and self-discovery.

Angry people are simply hurt people who are emotionally stunted. Somewhere along the way, they didn't grow emotionally like they needed to grow, so the angry inner child comes out from time to time—more often for some than for others. You can see this in people you know—and sometimes in yourself. Being aware of emotional immaturity and knowing what it looks like in yourself and in those around you can help you to handle things in a healthier, calmer way. Without this awareness, you can get stuck in a developmental rut. In fact, your whole life can get stunted when you don't know how to process emotions and handle anger. It can affect your job, family, and friends. This is the root cause of so many people's problems. They were stunted emotionally.

Until you are taught a better way, you will play out the childhood behaviors you learned. This could mean manipulating others to achieve your goals, using anger and aggression to get your way, playing small so as not to threaten others, and using your body to make others happy while disowning your true desires. The list of immature ways we process our feelings is endless.

If you have the capability to really dig deep and understand your emotions, you likely will find that there are motives and other emotions beneath them. We are essentially children living in adult bodies, expressing ourselves to the degree with which we matured emotionally.

Think about how children versus adults act when they are behaving in an emotionally immature manner:

EMOTIONALLY IMMATURE RESPONSE	CHILDREN	ADULTS
Avoidance	Flee when big feelings arise	Avoid difficult conversations
Blame	Blame the dog, siblings, or say "It wasn't me!"	Blame their boss, partner, or "the system"
Pouting / Withdrawal	Pout or sulk	Punish with silence
Attention-Seeking	Act out to get noticed	Post passive-aggressive content on social media or overshare for validation
Tantrums	Tantrum in the living room	Tantrum via text, road rage, or gossip
Emotional Repression	Say "I don't care!" when hurt	Say they're "fine" and distract with productivity or sarcasm
Escapism	Escape into play	Numb with consumption (TV, alcohol, shopping, etc.)
Regulation Needs	Need someone to calm them down	Expect partner or grown children to regulate their emotions
Fear of Abandonment	Yell "You don't love me anymore!"	Accuse others of abandonment or lash out when boundaries are set

If you find yourself doing any of these, first know you're not alone. This is everybody until they learn differently.

As you study and grow, emotionally and spiritually, each one of these behaviors can be replaced with healthy, emotionally mature alternatives. Below is a list of the emotionally immature responses adults exhibit from the chart above, with healthy alternatives that can be used to process emotions with self-awareness, self-responsibility, and integrity:

- **Avoiding difficult emotions:**
  Face discomfort with open-hearted communication.
  Prepare emotionally to have conversations that matter to you.
  Use "I" statements and commit to expressing yourself clearly rather than running away.
  - "This is hard to talk about, but I value honesty and connection, so I'm going to speak from my heart."

- **Blaming others without self-reflection:**
  Pause to reflect on your role in the situation.
  Take ownership where appropriate, even if others are also at fault.
  - "What is this situation trying to teach me about my patterns or expectations?"

- **Punishing with silence:**
  Communicate your need for space without shutting others out.
  Return to the conversation when you're ready.
  - "I need some time to process my feelings before we talk. I care about you and this conversation. I will come back when I am clear."

- **Posting passive-aggressive content or oversharing:**
  Turn inward for validation.
  Meditate, reflect, journal, or share vulnerably with someone you trust instead of posting online.
  - "What am I really craving right now? Is it attention, affirmation, connection? Can I give that to myself instead of seeking it externally?"

- **Venting through text, road rage, or gossip:**
  Learn to sit in the heat of your emotions.
  Find somewhere else to channel your energy, such as journaling, movement, or breathwork before dumping on others.
  - "I'm triggered right now. First, I will ground myself, then I will respond thoughtfully."

- **Pretending you're fine, using sarcasm:**
  Allow your true feelings to surface, and express them with honesty and compassion.
  - "That hurt, even though I brushed it off at first. I want to talk about it please."

- **Numbing with consumption (TV, alcohol, sex, shopping, etc.):**
  Meet your feelings where they are, with presence.
  Choose supportive outlets like meditation, journaling, body movement, walk in nature, or simply stillness.
  - "I notice my urge to numb. What feeling am I trying to avoid? Can I sit with it, if for just one minute?"

- **Expecting others to regulate your emotions:**
  Learn to self-soothe through various nervous system tools (breathwork, grounding, movement, etc.).
  Ask others for support, not to rescue you.
  - "I'm feeling overwhelmed. I'm going to take time to calm myself before I ask you for support."

- **Accusing others when they set boundaries:**
  Honor boundaries as your loved one's act of love and self-respect, for themselves and for you.
  Reflect instead of reacting.
  - "Their boundaries do not mean they are abandoning me. Their boundaries mean they want me in their life, or they would end the relationship. I can feel the sting of a boundary without retaliation and trust it is for the best."

Physical activity or movement can be helpful in the processing of our emotions. The beautiful thing about moving emotions through the body, whether it be through dance, exercise, walking, or even cleaning, is that you don't always have to mentally process what you're feeling. The body has a way of taking over and moving the emotions through you.

As a yoga instructor, I've experienced for myself and witnessed in others some substantial emotional releases during the practice of yoga. It's very common for people practicing yoga to begin sobbing or laughing as they tap into emotions that have been long stored within their body. If we don't move our bodies regularly in some way, these emotions can get stuck and can lead to major problems—mental and physical—depression, digestive issues, headaches, and other illness. Yoga is a gentle way to get the body moving and get the emotions flowing out of the body to provide improved health and well-being, as well as an enhanced mind-body-spirit connection.

I had been practicing yoga for almost ten years when one day I got into a certain pose and found myself sobbing. I knew it was best to let the emotions flow to prevent them from getting stuck and manifesting as disease. But some people don't know this, so they feel embarrassed and try to hold back the tears. This is where it's important to have a properly trained yoga instructor who understands the impact yoga has on emotions stored in the body. After the emotional release that day, I felt better than I had felt in years, and I've seen this happen for many other people too.

Sometimes we can also feel emotions well up during a massage or an acupuncture treatment. Maybe a tender spot being touched brings us to an emotional release.

Or we can simply have an experience that triggers an emotional reaction, like tearing up from a song, movie, reel, or commercial.

If you've ever experienced any of these emotional releases, you have already felt this profound truth in action. The body doesn't need your permission to feel. The body will naturally do its thing when given the proper environment, which paradoxically, can be movement, stillness, quiet, or simply space.

It is important to know that if you begin to experience an emotional release, it is best to let the emotions flow freely. If you stuff the emotions back down, you are essentially allowing imbalance to take hold. Once again, it's vital to understand that these emotions will make their way up to the surface one way or another. How much better is it to release them through yoga, massage, or healthy processing than allowing them to manifest in disease?

Identifying your emotions is a large step toward personal empowerment. Your emotions are not random, they are messengers. Each feeling is pointing to what matters most to you. Unidentified emotions can force you into reactive behavior. When you learn to recognize, classify, and process what you're feeling, you can respond from a place of awareness instead of reaction.

This emotional clarity will reduce self-sabotage. Rather than snapping at loved ones, shutting down, procrastinating, or numbing out, you interrupt the pattern by asking, "What am I really feeling right now?"

If you look around, you'll quickly notice that emotionally immature communication happens not just on individual levels but also as a society. Look at America—we are dealing with the same struggles in our country. Our media can be toxic, bent, and mentally controlling. We have a society out of touch with emotions and buying into the toxicity, which manifests in more and more anger…and less and less peace.

One interesting aspect of our society is that we are so distracted (and looking for more distractions all the time) that it gets in the way of our mind-body-spirit connection. This clearly plays a role in the anger we experience and see in the people around us. Being out of touch with emotions means we cannot process those emotions. But what might happen if we took the time and did the work to begin processing? What kind of impact could that have on our personal lives and in our society?

Empowerment is about choice. When you can identify and regulate your emotions, you are not ruled by them, but instead, you are guided by them. You gain the ability to choose your response, which is where your true power lies.

Once you've learned to identify your emotions, you unlock a deeper level of self-awareness, but emotional intelligence is only part of the equation. Beneath emotion lives something even older, more primal, and equally vital: instinct.

While emotions can guide you toward truth, your instincts often alert you before your mind can make sense of what is happening. Instinct is the body's raw, unfiltered wisdom; the internal compass that points toward safety, alignment, and empowerment.

The more you tune into both emotion and instinct, the more grounded and powerful you become. Let's explore how to reconnect with these instinctual signals and use them to reclaim your power.

CHAPTER 4

Instinct as a Sacred Guide

Animals have incredible instincts—we all know this. But we seem to forget that humans are animals too, although we tend to be very out of tune with our instincts.

What exactly are the benefits of utilizing instincts? Connecting with their instinctual intelligence, animals tie innate action to survival, protection, reproduction, and emotional expression. Consider the following instincts:

- Fight, flight, or freeze survival response – animals run from danger, attack when threatened, or play dead
- Territorial behavior – animals defend a home/nest and warn off intruders with growling, puffing up, standing tall
- Seeking safety and shelter – animals burrow or hide during a storm and return to a den or familiar space when injured or fearful
- Avoidance of harm – animals pull away from heat or sharp objects and refuse to eat something that smells "off" to them
- Comfort seeking – young animals nestle against a parent for warmth and soothing, and cry when separated
- Pack/tribe connection – animals herd other animals and tend to follow the group
- Self-soothing – cats purr or knead, dogs lick themselves when anxious, animals "shake it off" (quite literally) after a stressful encounter
- Nurturing and bonding – animals groom each other and protect offspring

But what about humans? Why don't we have these kind of instincts if we are animals too? The truth is we are born with these same strong instincts, and some carry into adulthood, but they get buried as we give away our power little by little over time. We have society, news, billboards, media, friends, and family telling us to believe ABC when our instincts are telling us to believe XYZ.

Remember the terrible tsunami of 2004? There were numerous reports of animals running away to safety before the wave hit the shores, while humans stood there and watched, fascinated by the water—many of those observers losing their lives. Animals followed their instincts; humans followed their need for entertainment and fulfillment of curiosity, or just had an inability to sense danger. The instinct to seek protection and survival was inactive.

As humans, we possess an innate response to danger that alerts us before our cognitive brains can process it. That instinct is there to protect us and save us. Because our instinct is continually ignored and discouraged by others, we no longer trust ourselves. Whether it's a tsunami, walking down a street we have a bad feeling about, or entering a relationship with someone who isn't good for us, we've silenced the instinct for so long that we put ourselves in grave danger—emotionally, mentally, and sometimes even physically.

Denying our instincts can put us in a number of relational problems that can make life difficult. When it comes to leaders, employers, lovers, or any number of people in your life, you should have an innate feeling about them one way or the other. If you experience the gut instinct that the person isn't good for you or isn't a wise person to trust, it's important to listen to that instinct.

Society may tell you otherwise, but if you ignore your instincts and follow what society says, you are giving away your power and your instinct becomes further and further out of reach. You are allowing what other people tell you to override your instinct. A person may fit what society deems as a "good person"—he or she may look the part (beautiful or attractive), say the right things, have the right job—but if your instinct is telling you this person is not good for you, you should listen.

If you do not listen to your instinct, you will realize down the road that listening in the first place could have saved you pain and heartache. You will also find that the more you allow the world (anyone who is NOT you) to tell you what you should be doing, the more difficult it becomes to trust yourself.

In my own life, I experienced this in regard to a dating relationship. I knew on the first date this guy wasn't right for me, even though he looked and acted perfect. Just prior to this first date, a friend told me my standards were too high, my clock was ticking, and I needed to quit being so picky or I would never find someone. I trusted this person and valued her opinion, so I gave it some serious consideration.

After the first date, I noticed a couple of red flags and told the guy I didn't think it was going to work. But he convinced me I was overreacting, that it was just an off night, a fluke, and we would make a great couple.

My instinct: Kick this guy to the curb and move on.

Outside messages: You need to quit being picky; your time is running out. This guy is perfect for you. So, you think you don't want to date me? You are wrong.

I silenced my instincts, denied what I knew was best for me, and continued in the relationship for two months, and it was a big mistake. I look back on that first date and realize I had the answer all along on this guy. Something inside of me knew he was wrong, and I was 100% right!

However, instead of following that instinct, I listened to the world. I internalized the messages from well-meaning (but wrong) loved ones telling me I needed to lower my standards and get in a relationship with someone. I second-guessed myself when I knew after the first date it should end and instead listened to this guy who was basically discrediting my instincts.

I was giving my power away to all these people instead of holding true to my instincts. We do this all the time, right? Kids are told to do whatever adults tell them to do. But there are times when children have gut instincts they absolutely need to trust.

Imagine a child who feels uneasy around a certain person or hides behind their parent in fear. That child is told "Be polite, say 'hi.' There is nothing to be scared of." We teach children that they cannot trust their own perception.

Or how about when we tell children to "finish your food, don't waste" when they say they're not hungry or stop eating when full.

These types of communication are prime examples of teaching children to deny their instincts. It may not seem like a big deal in many cases, but the children are establishing who they are, and when adults tell them to ignore their instincts, they begin to believe they can't trust themselves. Ignoring their instincts can continue to be a detrimental theme in their lives.

The possible consequences are children who internalize this denial of their instincts and become adults who gaslight themselves. This undermines intuition and creates adults who downplay or second-guess their gut feelings in dangerous or manipulative situations. Adults must help children be attuned to their instincts.

Again, I'm not saying we let kids do whatever they want, or we don't help them go outside their comfort zone. And we certainly should not let them manipulate in the name of their instincts. But we should help them assess what they are feeling and when to follow their instincts versus push themselves out of their own limitations.

Humans have dormant or underdeveloped instincts. With awareness, practice, and embodiment, we can reawaken these natural abilities. Reclaiming these instincts is empowering because it restores trust in our inner compass so we don't have to rely on external validation.

Consider some of the following human instincts that you can work to develop in support of your personal empowerment:

- **Intuitive knowing** – The ability to sense the truth before logic can explain it
    - Trusting your gut when something feels off, even when it "looks good on paper"
    - Sensing the energy of a person, place, or situation before there is physical proof
    - <u>To develop this instinct</u>: Practice decision-making from the body versus the mind.
    "How does this feel in my gut, heart, or body, not just my mind?"

- **Healthy aggression** – The instinct to assert, protect, and take up space (without causing harm)
    - Speaking up for your boundaries
    - Pursuing what you want without guilt
    - Defending your energy, time, or values
    - <u>To develop this instinct</u>: Practice speaking your truth, while maintaining kindness, on small things before moving to larger things. Be honest with yourself about how you want to spend your time, money, emotions. Move anger through the body and practice clear assertions.
    Physically stomp, punch a pillow, yell safely, growl, hum.

- **Self-regulation** – The instinct to return to internal balance after a stressful or stimulating event
    - Calming your nervous system without relying on someone or something else to help (people, alcohol, consumption)
    - Knowing how to soothe yourself during fear, rejection, or overwhelming situations
    - <u>To develop this instinct</u>: Learn self-regulation practices and practice them after small upsets, then work your way up to bigger events.
    Breathwork, grounding practices, shaking, rocking, stimming, humming, walking, cold water therapy

- **Embodiment sensation awareness** – The instinct to listen to the body's cues instead of ignoring or overriding them
    - Noticing tension, exhaustion, hunger, or excitement as messengers of the body
    - Using body feedback to guide decision-making around self-care
    - <u>To develop this instinct</u>: Check in with your body on a regular basis.
    "What sensations are present in my body right now? What are they trying to tell me?"

- **Rest and withdrawal cycles** – The instinct to retreat and replenish when necessary
    - Knowing when to pull back, say no, or simply go quiet
    - Honoring your cycles of rest and relaxation instead of pushing through exhaustion
    - <u>To develop this instinct</u>: Track your energy. Schedule "pause days." Normalize rest as power, not weakness.
    "I honor myself and my body by taking time to relax and recharge. I will be stronger and a 'better me' if I do."

- **Emotional expression** – The instinct to feel and release emotions instead of suppressing them
    - Crying when sad, shaking when scared, sighing when relieved, vocalizing your frustrations
    - Letting your feelings move through you, not get stuck inside of you
    - <u>To develop this instinct</u>: Let emotions rise, instead of pushing them down. Sit in meditation and scan your body if necessary.
    "I have found safe containers for emotional release (movement, art, rituals, talking to trusted people) and will utilize them."

- **Belonging without betrayal** – The instinct to find community without losing yourself in the process
    - Being part of something greater than yourself without abandoning your truth
    - Recognizing healthy versus performative connections
    - <u>To develop this instinct</u>: Practice speaking your truth in groups of safe people. Notice when fitting in costs too much.
    "I am safe to be myself in a group of people who support me. My honesty and true self are my gifts to the group."

- **Receiving** – The instinct to allow support, love, money, rest, and goodness to flow into your life
    - Letting yourself be helped, held, paid, and seen
    - Releasing guilt or fear around receiving
    - <u>To develop this instinct</u>: Practice saying "thank you" when given a compliment instead of deflecting. Notice and challenge blocks to receiving.
    "I deserve to be acknowledged, celebrated, and rewarded."

- **Discernment** – The instinct to sense what is aligned or misaligned (even subtly)
    - Knowing who you can trust, when to walk away, or when something is not aligned with your highest good
    - Knowing what is good for your body, including nutrition, movement, sleep, and other self-care practices
    - <u>To develop this instinct</u>: Notice patterns. Pay attention to early warning signs and red flags.
    Some examples of warning signs:
        - You feel tense, anxious, or drained after being around someone.
        - You feel like you need to defend yourself when with someone.
        - Someone dismisses or belittles you.

- You are pressured to say yes when your body is saying no.
- Someone's words and actions don't match.
- You feel rushed or panicked into making decisions.
- You feel a low level of dread rather than excitement when imagining the next step.
- You're tired after eating certain foods or drinking certain drinks but do them out of habit or social pressure.
- You feel tired or sore after specific workouts but push through anyway.
- You override your body's signals for rest, hunger, or stillness in favor of productivity or appearance.
- You absorb other people's moods or emotional weight.
- You have a strong desire to leave a room, exit a conversation, or change the subject.
- You feel consistently depleted in a specific environment, job, or relationship.

"If ever in doubt, I will pause before moving forward to check in with myself."

- **Noble Presence** – The instinct to lead with both your heart and spine
  - Standing rooted in your power without overpowering
  - Offering kindness and respect without collapsing or people-pleasing
    - <u>To develop this instinct</u>: Learn to hold boundaries without aggression and offer warmth without self-abandonment. Balance your confidence with humility. Speak truth with care.

"I don't need to raise my voice to stand in my truth. I'm not here to be loud, I'm here to be clear and lead with kindness."

The idea of noble presence is by far my favorite concept. True empowerment isn't loud or harsh, it is instead a noble presence. It is the instinct to speak and act with kindness and clarity, to move through life with grace. When power matures through the heart, this instinct will arise in you.

We will discuss some of the important tactics to nurture your sovereignty in the next chapter.

CHAPTER 5

Boundaries Without Bitterness

We all need to be able to hold boundaries and politeness at the same time. Honoring our instincts while showing kindness and compassion is a skill that takes a bit of practice and coaching to learn, but once mastered, it will benefit you for your entire life.

Boundaries will help your relationships thrive. If you don't have healthy boundaries, you could find yourself resenting others or feeling disappointed, violated, or taken advantage of. Most of the time people are not trying to overstep. They think differently than you and wouldn't mind if the roles were reversed. This is why we need to set clear boundaries, helping people know what we want or need.

Consider your needs and desires around your various types of boundaries:

- Physical
- Verbal
- Emotional
- Personal space
- Time
- Sexual
- Intellectual
- Material
- Workplace
- Family

Protecting your energy, needs, or values while still honoring connection and care with others is possible and highly recommended. In this way, you can honor your needs, while still attuning to others.

When communicating personal boundaries with those you care about, consider the following ways to do so with compassion:

- Utilizing "I" statements instead of "you" or blaming statements
- Validating the other person's feelings without compromising your truth
- Offering clarity and not excuses
- Using a firm and kind tone to match your intention

Practicing this will help you grow your skills around boundaries. Start with lower-stakes conversations and work your way up to high-stakes settings so you can master the skill before being faced with a momentous situation.

An area of life that requires colossal boundary setting, but also holds tremendous power, is the pursuit of your dreams, without guilt about what others think. This is one of the most radical acts of self-trust and empowerment. I say this as someone who has done it. My path to sole entrepreneurship—developing myself as an authority and expert in the field of wellness (two decades before anyone even understood what that term meant) and becoming an author—was questioned and ridiculed more than once.

Many of us have been conditioned to prioritize others' needs, play it safe, or stay small, but you can honor your desires without abandoning your integrity or important relationships.

The key theme around pursuing your dreams is that desire is not selfish. Guilt is often a sign you're breaking someone else's expectations, not that you are doing anything wrong. You can love others but still choose yourself.

No matter what type of boundaries you are enforcing, defending your energy while keeping your heart open is an important and empowering task. Holding your center without closing your heart leaves room for open, honest conversations that will grow your relationships while improving your life.

Here are some examples of ways you can set boundaries that are not cold or harsh but loving, self-respecting, and emotionally mature.

Declining Social Invitations Without Guilt

Scenario: A friend keeps inviting you to events, but you're not as sociable as she is. You're burnt out and need time for yourself.

Empowered Response: I really value our friendship, and I don't want you to feel ignored. I've been feeling super depleted lately and need some time to rest. Can we plan something low-key next week instead? Possibly just the two of us so we can have some quality one-on-one time.

Why it works: It honors the relationship, communicates your needs clearly, and offers a future connection point.

Setting Limits with Children Without Shame

Scenario: Your child wants to stay up late watching TV.

Compassionate Response: I know it's fun to keep watching, I understand that. But your body needs rest to feel its best tomorrow. Let's save the next episode for the weekend and do something cozy before bed.

Why it works: It holds the boundary while validating their feelings and maintaining connection.

Saying No at Work Respectfully

Scenario: A coworker asks you to take on extra tasks that aren't your responsibility.

Empowered Response: I want to support the team, and I know this is important. Right now, I am at capacity, and I would not be able to do it well. Can we look at other ways to get this covered?

Why it works: It acknowledges the request, respects the project, and protects your workload without blaming.

Not Answering Messages Immediately

Scenario: A friend or partner expects instant replies, but it overwhelms you.

Empowered and Compassionate Response: I love hearing from you, and sometimes I take a while to respond so I can give you my undivided attention. Just want you to know that it's not personal, it's how I manage my energy and time.

Why it works: It reassures them while modeling self-respect and emotional capacity.

Handling Family Pressure

Scenario: A family member pushes advice or opinions you didn't ask for.

Empowered Response: I know you're coming from a good place and I do appreciate that. Right now I am working on figuring this out on my own. I will reach out if I want to talk more about it.

Why it works: It affirms their good intent while clearly defining your need for emotional space.

Ending a Relationship with Integrity

Scenario: You've outgrown a friendship or relationship that has become unhealthy.

Empowered and Compassionate Response: This has been a meaningful connection for me, and I am grateful for it. But I have come to realize I need something different now to stay in alignment with who I am becoming. I wish you all the best.

Why it works: It honors the past, owns your truth, and exits with dignity instead of drama.

Managing Communication with a Co-Parent

Scenario: Your ex frequently texts or calls outside agreed-upon times, often with non-urgent issues, or in a tone that feels emotionally charged.

Compassionate Response: I want us to have a smooth co-parenting relationship for the sake of our child. To stay grounded and avoid unnecessary tension, I'd appreciate if we could stick to communicating only during our agreed-upon times unless it's an emergency. That way I can show up fully and calmly for the conversations that matter.

Why it works: It centers the shared goal of the child's well-being, avoids blame or emotional escalation, communicates what you need and why without cutting off communication, and allows space for healthy co-parenting to continue without codependency or emotional entanglement.

Choosing a Creative Career Over a "Safe" One

Scenario: You've worked in corporate for years but feel called to pursue art, writing, or healing work. Your family is worried you'll fail or go broke.

Empowered and Compassionate Response: I understand your concern, and I appreciate you looking out for me. I've spent a lot of time reflecting, and I know this path lights me up in a way nothing else does. I have formulated a plan to take this leap responsibly. I hope you can support me even if it looks different than what you imagined.

Why it works: You acknowledge their concern but don't ask for permission. You own your dream with clarity and care.

Moving to a New City or Country for Growth

Scenario: You're offered an incredible opportunity that would require moving away from family or friends who are disappointed or guilt-tripping you.

Empowered Response: This move feels aligned with what I am building for myself. I will miss being close, but I know I am growing into the person I am meant to be. I hope you'll cheer me on, even from a distance.

Why it works: It acknowledges connection but centers sovereignty.

Opting Out of Draining Conversations

Scenario: A friend or family member constantly complains, gossips, or emotionally dumps.

Empowered and Compassionate Response: I want to support you, and I also notice I feel really drained after these conversations. Can we focus on things that leave us both feeling stronger or maybe take a break from this topic for now?

Why it works: You protect your energy field while still offering connection.

Protecting Your Parenting Values with Family

Scenario: A relative gives your child candy, media, or messaging that goes against your values.

Compassionate Response: I know you're trying to treat them and be loving, and I love that! We're choosing a different approach for now because it's so important to us. I'd appreciate your support while we're working through it.

Why it works: You avoid shaming them, explain the "why," and firmly restate your boundary.

Living Your Truth Around Differing Beliefs

Scenario: You hold spiritual, political, or lifestyle beliefs that your family disagrees with.

Empowered Response: I know we see things differently, and I respect your right to your view. I'm not looking to convince you, but I am also not going to silence what matters to me. Let's agree to disagree and stay in relationship.

Why it works: You stay rooted in your values without trying to dominate or disengage.

The beauty of all these responses is that you do not have to choose between being kind and being clear. Defending your time, energy, and values can be an act of love, for yourself and for others.

It is normal and healthy to disagree. The goal is to disagree with love and with the idea of unifying yourself with others, not separating yourself from them. Using disagreement to express yourself, but also as a tool to stay in relationship with others and your authentic self, will lead to ultimate freedom for all.

Keep an open mind and an open heart, share your truth, and invite unity at the end.

I started this chapter talking about how most people do not mean to disregard your boundaries, they simply are not clear in understanding them. These are people who you have a certain amount of respect and reciprocity with, and they are willing to respect your requests.

However, it is possible that you have people in your life that consistently overstep boundaries, interfere in your life, and are full of destructive habits that negatively affect you. These people will not stop with a simple response, explanation, or discussion, as in the examples so far. They will continue pushing and force you to act upon your boundaries.

Here's the thing: Often, people think of boundaries as something they force upon others. Boundaries are not about others. Boundaries are not about forcing others to change, controlling them, or telling them how to behave. Boundaries are about you, about what happens after you make a request for someone to change, and they decide not to. The boundary is what you decide to do after they have disrespected your rules.

For example, let's say you have someone in your life who communicates with aggression and this upsets you. You have asked this person to find more healthy communication styles and not raise his voice to you. You've explained kindly and compassionately that this bothers you and makes you feel extreme anxiety, throwing you off for days following the event. This person continues to scream and yell, having breakdowns and tantrums when he is upset with you.

What you do now is your boundary.

You cannot stop him from behaving this way. You cannot force him to change or control him; he is an adult. But you can decide your next steps.

You may tell him if he does this, you will walk out of the room. If he follows you, you will leave the house. If he follows you again, you will call the police. These are your boundaries.

Hopefully the situation will resolve when you walk out of the room, and you two can come together to discuss the situation later when he has calmed down. Hopefully you don't need three stages because the situation doesn't keep escalating. But having these steps laid out will help you to decide how to handle yourself in the moment, should it occur.

These people can be super triggering, and these situations could bring up difficult emotions within you. We have already started talking in a previous chapter about managing your emotions, but it could also be helpful to find some outside help to deal with these types of situations. People like this can be toxic to your life and bring all kinds of mental and emotional problems to you.

While boundaries are your responsibility to maintain, sometimes an outside voice is helpful in navigating the situation. Should this be a respected and well-educated friend in this area, a therapist, or even a religious/spiritual teacher, finding a confidant to discuss the specifics of your circumstances with could help you emotionally and mentally.

CHAPTER 6

Truth Without Illusion: Seeing Others Clearly

I am a strong believer in having teachers and getting guidance from people and groups who can help us grow mentally, emotionally, spiritually, and in faith. I have many powerful teachers, in various walks of faith. But I believe it is far past time we start asking questions before we blindly follow others. You can begin now to tap into your inner strength, your instinct, and begin to see that people are flawed and not all can be trusted completely—you certainly don't need to allow what they say about you to override your own instincts.

Over the years, I have made many friendships in the self-help world. God bless them! Many of these leaders are wonderful people and good at what they do. They know how to talk the right talk, but some of them (not most, but some) are absolute disasters behind closed doors. I mean, unbelievably screwed up, studying self-help in desperation to help themselves. I watch some of these leaders post things on social media and it makes me very concerned. Their followers are asking them for coaching, trusting them with their lives, turning to them for the answers. Meanwhile, some of these coaches are struggling to keep their heads above water.

We should all know by now that people can put one image up on social media and live an entirely different life in reality. But it's easy to forget this when it comes to leaders—especially those in the self-help world. People give their power away to unhealthy and unwise leaders all the time.

Years ago, I was at a well-known self-help conference in Toronto. I was walking through, checking out various booths and displays, when I noticed a guy looking very yoga elite, walking around in all white. I got a closer look and realized he was stopping people and telling them that he was reading their soul. He was giving unsolicited advice to everyone he encountered.

I watched him intently and he noticed me. He stopped my friend and me. He glared at her, saying, "You are sick with disease. You have so much disease in you!" Although we were both pretty surprised at his nerve, it didn't faze either of us…we were both confident, and certain he was a whack. We just looked at him, smirked, and walked away. We watched as he continued to move from person to person, "reading their souls." It was shocking how many people were buying into his quackery.

It turned out he was a speaker at that conference and somewhat famous in that community.

People at these events are often in bad spots in their lives, just desperate for answers and willing to give their power away to anyone who can advise them on what in the heck to do to change their situation. They have completely lost touch with their instincts and don't even consider that they should be turning inward for answers instead of asking this crazy yogi-wannabe wearing all white.

You see this same story in various places, don't you? People give their power away more often than they realize. They give their power to people or systems that appear authoritative, impressive, or influential. Authority figures like politicians, physicians, religious leaders, spiritual gurus, bosses, CEOs, and teachers are commonly handed blind power. Cultural idols like celebrities, influencers, public figures, wealthy people and entrepreneurs, lifestyle gurus, and motivational speakers can also be included in this mix.

Personal relationships can also strip someone of their power, whether with romantic partners, parents, siblings, friends, or peer groups. We give our power away every time we believe that someone else's voice, validation, or authority matters more than our own.

If you find yourself in a position of giving too much power to anyone, it's always a good idea to stop yourself and really assess the situation, asking a few important questions:

- What do you know about this person that has led you to believe you can trust him or her?
- How is this person more qualified to give you advice than you are to know what is best for you?
- What does your gut instinct tell you about this person when you step back and take a careful look at what he or she is saying and doing?
- Am I seeking this person's approval because I don't trust my own inner guidance?
- Do I feel smaller, confused, or less worthy after interacting with this person?
- Am I afraid something might happen if I disagree with this person?
- Am I making this person more powerful in my mind than they actually are?
- Has this person earned the influence I've given them, or did I hand it over (possibly out of habit, fear, or hope)?
- If I truly trusted myself, would I still be seeking this person's opinion, approval, or permission?
- Does this person benefit from me staying unsure of myself, dependent upon them, or small in any way?
- When I imagine setting a boundary with this person, do I feel empowered or terrified?
- Am I confusing charisma or confidence with actual wisdom or integrity?

These questions are not about judging others. Instead, they are about remembering that your power is not up for outsourcing. Discernment is a healthy form of respect and responsibility.

I know it can feel unnatural to ask these questions and go through this process, but it is important work, especially if you have lived your life giving your power away to others. If listening to your instincts feels unnatural or foreign, you will need to PRACTICE until it begins to feel more comfortable.

Although I made a practice of giving my power away to others—doctors, leaders, friends, family members—for some of my childhood, once I started working on taking back my power, I could see such figures much more clearly. The people who had held this power and influence over me started to seem…well, normal. Just flawed people trying to figure things out. Not people worthy of my complete trust and obedience!

But until you start the process of questioning those around you with healthy discernment, this can be an issue. This is necessary not only in the self-help industry but also in the religious world, the medical community, and political realms. So many leaders and self-proclaimed experts are in fact actors, and people give their power to them all the time. It's a dangerous thing.

When it comes to the medical community, it's easy to see how this blind following happens. People are fearful. They get a bad diagnosis. We don't teach people to take care of themselves, so they follow whatever the person in a white coat tells them to do. They don't have the ability or confidence to educate themselves and learn what to do. So they go down whatever treatment path is suggested, and then sometimes show up on a holistic practitioner's doorstep as a last resort, because what they have been doing isn't working.

What if instead of blindly doing whatever some medical professional tells you to do, you sit in meditation and ask your body what it needs?

Maybe the medical professional is correct, and it is the best path. Maybe not. Giving yourself a chance to contemplate it, in silence, in communication with your higher self, is a powerful tool to develop and utilize in those situations.

As part of a former job, I used to run flu shot programs for employers and companies. The objective was to keep employees healthy and working during flu season. While I think the flu shot can be good for some people, I do not think it is good for all. For myself, I prefer not to take the flu shot. But I believe there are some who benefit from it, such as the immune compromised, elderly, and people who are traveling a lot or susceptible for whatever reason.

Anyway, at these clinics, I was the front-line person, and people would come up to me and ask, "Should I get the flu shot?" They were asking *ME* to make this important, personal decision for them, and they didn't know me at all. They had no idea of my credentials, my personality or communication style, whether I respected medical autonomy, or if I had a hidden agenda of any kind. (For goodness' sake, I was the face person at a flu shot clinic. It was very possible I was being rewarded for high numbers of vaccinations!)

Instead of giving them an answer, I would ask them if they had done any research on the topic to help them make their decision. Usually, the answer was no. So often I would advise them to go back to their seats or desks and do a bit of research. I told them even thirty minutes of research on the pros and cons of the flu vaccine would suffice. Then, I told them to meditate, to take ten deep breaths and then ask their bodies if they should get the vaccination once their mind was settled. I would suggest that they should get a strong answer one way or the other.

Nearly everyone I had this discussion with would come back with a strong answer. (Even those who decided against it came back to thank me for the guidance, as they learned a powerful new tool.) They didn't need an answer from me, or a mandate from someone else… they needed to educate themselves and then listen to their bodies for the answer that was right for them.

There have been far too many examples of people ignoring their gut instinct that the flu shot was wrong for them or for their child, and then they experienced terrible disorders or side effects as a result of going through with it. Something like the flu shot should be considered on a case-by-case basis and should be a personal decision.

It's difficult to find medical practitioners who will allow you to have this kind of freedom under their care. I am so fortunate to have a dear friend named Annette who is a dermatologist. She allows me some personal time to take deep breaths and meditate before making decisions about spots to be removed and other procedures. She honors my instincts. This is how medicine should be. You may have to spend some time searching to find doctors who will work with you in this way, but it's well worth the effort to find them. They are out there!

Of course, I feel like it's important to clarify that there is a fine line when making these kinds of decisions medically. If you aren't completely attuned to your body, medical situations are not the time to practice. For example, I'm not going to tell someone who was diagnosed with Stage 4 cancer to listen to their body to decide if they should have life-saving interventions, especially if they don't feel confident when it comes to listening to self.

Start small with seeking your instincts in your everyday life—not life-or-death situations. Don't just start listening to yourself when the decision is huge. You may not have the ability to truly be in tune. Build your practice of asking self in small matters over time so you will be ready when more major decisions need to be made.

How often have you found yourself saying "I knew it deep down" but you chose to ignore your gut feeling? If you strengthen that muscle, you will be far more likely to trust yourself in the future and, rather than looking to solve your problems, you will be able to avoid them altogether.

Before we move on, I encourage you to take a few moments to go through the checklist below and pick at least one area to work on. This is how you can exercise your instincts, which will move you forward on the path to taking back your power.

- Can you think of specific times during your childhood in which you were taught to let an adult figure or leader override your instincts? Spend some time writing about this experience, or share it with a friend you trust. Why did you allow this? What emotions were you experiencing? What would you tell that child in that moment today, knowing what you know now?

- List people in your life now who may try to take away your power and override your instincts. What do they do? How do you feel when you are around them? Identify what you can do to decrease their influence in your life. Can you envision them as an insecure child, trying to control as a mechanism to feel safe? How would you handle that child?

- Think of situations in which you might be able to practice your "instinct muscle"—the muscle that enables you to listen to self. Think of scenarios and consider how you can respond in a way that gives you the time and space to listen to self instead of blindly following what someone else tells you.

- Take a few minutes to practice "listening" to self. Meditate. Close your eyes and breathe deeply for ten breaths—inhale, exhale. Quiet your thoughts and settle your mind, and then ask yourself a question. It could be a question like "Should I go to this upcoming conference or skip it?" Or "Should I ask for a raise at my job?" Whatever the question is, take time to meditate on it and ask yourself for the answer. By practicing this process, you will strengthen your muscle and become more attuned to your instincts.

It is also important to note that finding people who build you up is one of the most empowering things you can do for yourself. Sometimes you meet someone and immediately know you will be lifelong friends. There are leaders, physicians, and teachers that you instantly have a strong connection with. These people are diamonds in the rough, gems to be treasured and trusted. If someone makes you feel safe, loved, and like you can accomplish anything, hold onto these people tight! They are your tribe, and they deserve to be cherished.

CHAPTER 7

Intuition Speaks: Will You Listen?

We all have an inner voice (or intuition) that speaks to us in normal everyday moments and helps guide us. Developing attunement to your intuition is important because it strengthens your ability to navigate life from within, rather than constantly seeking direction from the outside. By doing this, you will make choices with clarity that align with your values, needs, and inner truth.

This connection protects you from manipulation and gives you greater confidence in your decisions. It allows you to pause and listen to that little voice inside. It helps you build self-trust. And when you trust yourself, you can live your life with conviction, even in uncertain times.

But external voices (family, friends, media, societal "shoulds") can drown this voice out. Moving too fast through life will make you miss subtle signals. Overthinking can harm this connection. When the mind is busy speaking too loudly, the inner voice cannot be heard.

Numbing out the body and mind can seriously impair this connection. We do this all the time, with so many mediums. The phone, TV, and social media are possibly the top culprits, but there are more obvious ones like drugs and alcohol. Of course, many do it with work, which is often the easiest to justify.

Learning your inner voice is an important tool in personal empowerment. Your inner voice doesn't compete with anything. It's like a frequency that is always there, just waiting for you to get quiet enough to hear it.

To do this, I suggest practicing stillness. Sit in silence (without any media or outside input), even if only for five minutes a day. Set your timer if you'd like. Let your thoughts settle and watch what arises beneath them.

This is how you'll connect to the quiet voice inside of you that already knows everything. This isn't the voice of fear, ego, or conditioning. This is the deeper voice beneath it all that acts as your personal compass. This is the voice that knows when something is off; the voice that knows the answers before your brain can explain why. It exists to guide you to and through your personal life path. The path that is perfectly designed for you to learn the lessons you came here to learn.

Blending intuition, your body's wisdom, and your emotional truth, this voice will tell you what literally no one else can: how to move forward in life to achieve your life's mission and goals. How could anyone else ever know that truth besides you? It is your life, your destiny, your calling. Without inner attunement, you could disconnect from that inner voice, override your truth in favor of "logic," and head down the completely wrong path.

This isn't about hearing a booming divine voice but about learning to notice, trust, and follow the quiet voice inside of you. The more you listen to the little things, the louder your truth becomes in the bigger things.

Two of the overarching themes in the practices are stillness and body-led decision-making.

Learning to listen to yourself will bring confidence that is otherwise difficult to foster. The more you trust your inner guidance, the less you seek permission from outside forces. As you strengthen this muscle, you will be so certain of your decisions and life direction, it simply won't matter what anyone else thinks. This is confidence that brings resilience, power, and clarity in chaos.

Your intuition will have a language of its own, which you will start to know as it shows itself. Synchronicities that keep repeating in your life are most likely your inner voice trying to communicate with you.

Watch closely for opportunities being offered to you as you approach new ways of thinking. There are a million ways this could play out. The key is to be open and receptive when new things show up.

Some examples of synchronicities include running into someone after thinking about them; questioning new subjects to study or classes to attend only to find a flyer for those exact classes on a table; thinking about looking for new work and then someone offers you a new job unexpectedly. You may open a completely new avenue for yourself through some of these sources, meeting new people and solidifying new practices that could be life changing.

Often when there is music or TV on in the background as I am talking with someone, I will say an important phrase or word in a sentence, then the same phrase or word will pop up in the media I am listening to or will literally be on a street sign/billboard as I drive. I will immediately notice that synchronicity and feel a sense of expansion or constriction in my body. These are literal signposts trying to grab my attention. They are usually signs drawing me toward or away from something.

That gut feeling to explore is a language of the soul. Pay attention when you get a tug in the belly or a strong draw to check something out. That is your intuition trying to communicate with you.

Here are some intuition builders to help you get started:

- What should I wear today to feel most comfortable?
    - Notice how you feel throughout the day.
- What do I want to eat right now?
    - Notice how your body feels afterward (satisfied, sluggish, energized, relaxed, wired).
- Which item on this restaurant menu feels most aligned?
    - Close your eyes and listen to your body's subtle pull.
- Do I need to rest or move right now?
    - Ask this in the middle of the day and feel the truth in your body.

- Should I take this route or that one to my destination?
    - Observe whether the road felt calm, chaotic, delayed, or easy.
- Which grocery checkout line should I choose?
    - Pick the one your body leans toward, not the "logical" shortest line, and see what happens.
- What email or message should I respond to first?
    - Pause, let your eyes scan your inbox. Notice which name or subject line "lights up" your body. Trust it.
- Do I actually want to go to this event or am I saying "yes" from guilt or habit?
    - Ask, feel, decide. Then reflect after the event on whether your choice nourished you or depleted you.
- Which item/piece of clothing should I get rid of?
    - Hold each item and ask yourself: "Does this carry vitality or dead energy?" Let your body decide.
- Who should I check in with today (if anyone)?
    - Ask: "Is someone pulling at my awareness for a reason?" Then reach out. Notice what happens.
- What time should I go to bed tonight to feel my best tomorrow?
    - Try listening one night, ignoring it the next. Compare how you feel.
- Where should I sit in the room to feel most clear?
    - Scan your options with your body. Don't overthink it. Notice how you feel.
- What do I need right now that I haven't admitted to myself?
    - Sit in silence, ask inwardly. Wait for a word, image, feeling, or knowing to arise.

Starting small, by asking your intuition questions like these, will allow you to build trust with yourself and your innate knowledge. The more you listen to the little things, the louder your truth becomes in the bigger things.

If your intuition doesn't open up easily, journaling can help you move past your inner critic to let out the truth. Simply sitting down with a blank sheet of paper and writing anything that comes to mind is a great way to get the creative juices flowing. Try for three pages, without stopping or censoring yourself.

If you need a prompt, try one of these:

- If I were completely honest with myself, I would say....
- What do I need to know most right now?
- What truth is inside of me, asking to come out?
- Reveal what has been buried or hidden.
- Where in my life have I overridden my inner voice? And what was the result?
- When have I listened to my inner voice and been grateful that I did?
- What does my inner "yes" feel like? What does my inner "no" feel like?
- What environments help me hear myself more clearly? What dulls the connection?
- How does my inner voice speak to me (feeling, sound, imagery, dreaming, knowing, etc.)?
- When have I denied my inner voice and regretted it?

You can also simply have a conversation with your inner self. Sometimes this is easier to write than to do aloud or quietly in your mind.

Write a conversation between "you" and your higher self, inner child, or true self. Let each voice speak freely. If it is difficult to get started, try a prompt like "Dear inner child, what have you been wanting to tell me?" You might be astonished by what comes out. Often the most surprising thoughts hold the deepest truth.

Your intuition could use your dreams or other types of imagery to gain your attention. Recurring dreams or imagery in nature are both powerful pulls for our attention. Dreams are elusive and may need interpretation, as they often reflect repressed or subconscious thoughts. You may find your dreams have symbols or recurring themes.

Dreams leave us fast; journaling is best done first thing upon waking. I find my dreams make zero sense as I am remembering them first thing in the morning, but after I journal them, they tend to become clearer. I can see patterns emerge when practicing this often.

You may realize your dreams include loved ones who have passed. Are you simply remembering them? Honoring them? Or are they trying to communicate something to you? Dreams involving loved ones can be especially profound in delivering meaning.

If you are not remembering your dreams and you want to, consciously meditate before you go to sleep or ask your subconscious to remember them just before you go to bed. In your meditation, command yourself: "Show me tonight, in my dreams, what I am not seeing clearly."

Witnessing nature can be an intuitive practice for connecting with your innermost thoughts. To do this, simply sit quietly with a natural element (example: a tree, body of water, animal, or the wind). Ask it (or ask spirit through it) any of the following prompts:

- What have you been wanting to tell me?
- What are you here to show me about myself?
- How can you guide me to get in touch with my inner thoughts and feelings?
- What can I do to help my life improve?

Journal or listen to the sounds of nature speaking to you. Take note of your feelings and intuition; they will speak louder than anything. Don't analyze—just feel.

All the above exercises can be written or spoken. Using a voice recording app will let your voice flow so you don't have to write or type quickly. If that is your preferred method, listen back to the recordings and pay attention to the following to reveal deeper truths:

- What is your tone?
- Are there any hesitations?
- Are there any passionate moments?

There are so many exercises that have the potential to connect us to our intuition. I once attended a retreat in Florida where they were teaching us how to trust our intuition. One evening, they paired us up and told us to use our intuition to get to our restaurant of choice. We had to choose the restaurant and then get there without any directions or address.

Mind you, this was a new area to me, so I had no idea where the restaurant was. Instead, my partner and I had to go internal, ask ourselves questions, and decide which direction to go at every turn to arrive at our destination. We would literally come to a stoplight and decide what our intuition was telling us about the next turn. And we made it—before we knew it, we were in front of the correct restaurant! We were so tuned in from being at the retreat and practicing deep meditation that we were very aligned and balanced and could easily hear and trust our internal voices to get us where we needed to be that night.

This is very similar to how I felt when I decided what path to take following my Crohn's disease diagnosis. I had a very strong internal knowledge that showed me what to do. Even when medical professionals were telling me otherwise, I knew I needed to go a different route to treat my illness. I didn't know exactly what to do, but my intuition clearly told me that their advice was not good for my body, and I should seek out another treatment option.

Sometimes the internal knowing doesn't make perfect sense and may even seem a little crazy. You just know you need to do something and then trust that it will all make sense on the other side. At times like this, it is important to focus on being balanced and aligning your mind-body-spirit so you can tap into your intuition confidently and trust it. (We will talk more about how to do this in upcoming chapters.)

Don't worry about what others are saying or how they are judging you. If you are attuned, you can safely trust your intuition.

Your inner voice is always with you and always available. It is begging you to slow down and listen. It is not mysterious, it doesn't demand perfection; instead, it is always guiding and finding new ways to reach you. Your relationship with your personal wisdom will be unshakable once you commit to it. But it will take an ongoing commitment and practice for it to stay strong. If you do that, it won't matter what other people see or think. All that will matter is that you stay attuned.

And, if all else fails, your higher self will use your body as a messenger of its communication.

CHAPTER 8

Your Body Never Lies

When we don't quiet down enough to hear our intuition or slow down enough to listen to our inner voice, it finds another way to get our attention: through the body. Discomfort, pain, and tension are often messages, not just symptoms.

When you start to accept that your physical experience is simply revealing deeper truths, you will quickly want to learn how to listen so it can guide you back into alignment.

I started down this path decades ago when I picked up a book by Louise Hay called *Heal Your Body: The Mental Causes for Physical Illness and the Metaphysical Way to Overcome Them*, which went into great detail about what ailments correlate to what mental blockages. She was a motivational author and leader in the self-help movement, far beyond her years.

The concept of every physical ailment having a corresponding mental cause shaped much of my spiritual foundation and how I learned to communicate with myself. I bought into the concept and started listening to what my soul was telling me through my body. It was powerful and helped me overcome many physical challenges, as I've already shared with you.

At first, I remember reading her book and looking up the physical challenges of others. They were spot on! I mean, dead on. People I knew who had breast problems were in fact, like her book said, putting everyone else before themselves and taking care of themselves last. People who had bone breaks were in fact, like her book said, rebelling against authority. People with constipation did have a difficult time releasing old ideas and were often stuck in the past. People with low back pain did say they felt unsupported. People with throat issues did have difficulty speaking their truth. People with stomach issues were unable to digest their emotions or situations. And so on…

But, for some reason, when I looked up my ailments, they didn't resonate.

Interesting, isn't it? This woman had all this wisdom that correlated perfectly to everyone else's physical ailments, but not to mine. How odd.

Then it hit me; my ego was stopping me from seeing the truth.

I remember realizing that if this book and its information could be so obviously applied to everyone else, it must be true for me too. If I could just accept the information as truth, no matter how much my ego was telling me otherwise, I could work on the problem, fix it, and move past it.

So that is what I did. I took this book as bible and decided to look up every single physical issue I had, no matter how small, and start on a journey to correct the mental process associated with it.

And when I did this, my life catapulted forward.

There are many ways you can tap into your body's communication system. Reading books like this, learning to hear your body's voice through meditation and journaling, and developing relationships with health professionals that can guide you in the proper direction are all options.

Another widely known and used tool is biofeedback. If the body already knows the answers, maybe there is a way to access the answers, rather than waiting for the imbalances to manifest in physical ailments.

Biofeedback is a method of gaining awareness and control over your body's automatic functions by using signals from your own physiology. It helps you listen to what your body is saying in real time so you can self-regulate and create balance.

Think about all the ways your body communicates with you:

- Breath awareness – noticing changes in your breathing patterns during decisions, stress, or emotion.
- Nervous system cues – observing physical sensations (tightness, heat, nausea, trembling, expansion, ease) that tell you what's safe, what's triggering, or what's unresolved.
- Postural biofeedback – standing tall, taking up space, and expanding is a sign of confidence and comfort, while crossing arms, slouching, and shrinking is a sign of uncertainty and insecurity.
- Heart rate coherence – observing one's heart rhythm can reveal physiological alignment or misalignment, as well as calm and focused states.
- Goose bumps, tears, shivers – these powerful, primal confirmation signals of the body can signify truthful, inspiring, or aligned moments.
- Gut feelings – the gut has been dubbed the "second brain" and it reacts before your mind does with butterflies, nausea, or tightening—clues from your body's emotional center.
- Body scanning meditation – using this mindfulness tool builds awareness of subtle physical and emotional shifts, which is useful for stress mapping and intuitive decision-making.
- Dream signaling – observing the subconscious processing of unresolved tension, intuition, or inner truth through dream interpretations.

Any time we use the physical body to interpret what is going on in the mind, we are using biofeedback tools. A few examples that are commonly used in mainstream medicine are:

- Heart rate monitors / EKG (electrocardiogram) – measures electrical signals in the heart

- EEG (electroencephalogram) – measures electrical activity in the brain
- Respiratory biofeedback (spirometry) – measures breathing rate, lung function, and oxygen flow
- Skin temperature feedback – measures micro-changes in skin temperature, often used in stress testing
- EMG (electromyography) – measures muscle activity via surface electrodes
- Galvanic skin response (electrodermal activity) – measures skin conductivity and sweat gland activity
- Heart rate variability devices – measures the variation between heartbeats, which are an indicator of nervous system balance
- Continuous glucose monitors – measures blood sugar response to stress, food, and lifestyle choices in real time
- Blood pressure monitors – measures blood pressure, which can be used to assess how rest, stress, and lifestyle affect pressure
- Functional MRIs – measures brain activity as it occurs, based on blood pressure flow

While tests like these measure physical processes in the body, what they're often revealing is the impact of what is happening in the mind. That's because our thoughts, emotions, and mental stressors directly affect how our nervous system, heart, muscles, and breath behave. The mind communicates through the body, so when stress, anxiety, overthinking, or emotional suppression occur, they show up physiologically. These tools give us a window into that connection by measuring how the body responds to what is happening in our inner world, even when we are not consciously aware of it.

Another powerful biofeedback tool that we have available to us is muscle testing.

What is muscle testing? It's like a lie detector test, or better yet, a personal truth detector. While ego can convince our minds that reality is false and vice versa, muscle testing can reveal the truth (whether you know the truth in your mind or not). Muscle testing allows you to develop your intuition and use your body to know what you know, so to speak. Accessing your intuition can be difficult in a world where we are bombarded with outside noise. Muscle testing can help you as you begin to become physically and spiritually attuned.

Muscle testing, known as applied kinesiology, came about in the 1960s thanks to Dr. George Goodheart, who was the first to use manual muscle testing to find a weak muscle and then employ chiropractic techniques to strengthen the muscle. He then looked beyond the chiropractic field to biomedicine, acupuncture, osteopathy, dentistry, nutrition, and biochemistry for methods to strengthen weak areas of the body, thus increasing the health and well-being of his patients.

This method of diagnosis and treatment is based on the belief that various muscles are linked to particular organs and glands and that specific muscle weakness can signal distant internal problems, such as nerve damage or chemical imbalances. By correcting the muscle weakness, the patient can receive healing. We also use applied kinesiology to diagnose and treat nervous system problems, nutritional issues, and imbalances in the body.

Goodheart was the forerunner of using the body itself as a diagnostic tool in this way. Today, chiropractors, acupuncturists, osteopaths, kinesiologists, and many other practitioners can perform muscle testing to help people with self-discovery and improved health and well-being. The premise of *how* muscle testing works for our purposes of self-empowerment includes:

- When you lie and lack integrity, you lose your strength.
- Being honest with yourself and others (integrity) is a significant part of owning your strength, building your strength, and empowering yourself.

Have you ever stopped to consider how we underestimate the power of lies? They may seem harmless, but lying can weaken the body's entire system. If you undergo muscle testing, you will quickly see how your muscles are not as strong when you tell a lie.

In fact, studies have revealed that when you tell a lie, your body will only have 85% of its usual strength. It's like instant karma! When you lie, you are literally weakening your body's system. When you tell the truth, you are strengthening your body's system. Furthermore, truthfulness with oneself and others is the path to unlocking intuition.

Whether your issue is lying, negative thinking, or another damaging activity, you need to view your body like a power grid that is either receiving power or giving power away. Your power grid can help you to achieve healthy relationships, finances, and physical states. You can charge up the power in your grid with activities that drive connectedness, such as being truthful, being kind to others, self-care, meditation, and rest. But you use up power when you lie, harm yourself or others, and live in a way that is not positive or healthy. You will eventually run out of power if you are continually depleting it without filling it back up.

Not only can muscle testing reveal to you the importance of living an authentic life and being true to yourself, but it can also help you make decisions of all kinds. You can muscle test on small things—like "What would be best to wear today?" or "What should I eat?"…or on big things like "Should I take this job?" or "Should I choose this person as a mate or business partner?"

Many practitioners use it for identifying the right supplements and treatments for their patients. They might have the person hold the supplement in one hand or under their chin with their other arm out at shoulder height. From there, they will test that arm muscle to determine which supplement brings the strongest and weakest reaction. The stronger muscle reaction points to the best supplements for that individual…just like the stronger muscle reaction points to the truth.

Muscle testing can be difficult to do on your own, but there are self muscle testing techniques and tutorials available online if you're interested in trying it yourself. I will explain my process below if you care to attempt it.

To practice muscle testing yourself, you need to be calm, clear, and neutral about the subject. Often, we desire a certain answer, which will make it easy to override the body's natural response. Beginners often unintentionally sway results by focusing too much on what they hope is true. You can also have a dysregulated nervous system already, maybe due to stress or being tired or emotionally charged. This will make the signal less clear. Beginners also struggle to interpret the subtle changes in muscle resistance.

Here are some tips to get you started:

- To calibrate your responses, start with yes/no questions that you already know the answer to.
- Ask from a neutral place. Take a breath, relax, and try not to influence the outcome.
- Practice daily and track patterns to build trust in your body's signals.
- Use self muscle testing as guidance not gospel. It is a tool not a final verdict, especially if you are new to the process.

I like asking a friend to test me while I direct the process. This is my process:

- I hold my arm straight out to my side, raised to shoulder height.
- I keep my arm strong in that position and ask my friend to push down on it. This establishes baseline strength.
- I then say a true statement, such as "My name is Cassie Sobelton."
- I ask my friend to push down again. (My strength is still as strong as the baseline here.)
- I then state a false statement, for example "My name is Jackie Hillard."
- Again, I ask my friend to push down. (My strength typically breaks under pressure when stating a lie and my arm falls.)

- If this goes as expected, I know my body is communicating truth.
- If not, or if I just need further assurance, I state more true/false statements and ask my friend to push down after each.
- Only once I feel certain that my body is communicating truths and lies properly do I move forward with my questions.

Ideally, and especially for medical issues, you'd have the help of a practitioner, but trialing this on your own and learning your body in this way is a fun and empowering practice.

Your body is constantly communicating with you, but most people were never taught its language. Because of this, those people think disease is random, a natural part of aging, or simply genetics.

When you begin the work to learn to communicate with yourself and increase the level of trust you have for yourself, there is one important word that comes to mind. It's a complicated word, but it's important to have a basic understanding of it: **Epigenetics.**

From the website WhatIsEpigenetics.com:

> Epigenetics is the study of heritable changes in gene expression (active versus inactive genes) that does not involve changes to the underlying DNA sequence — a change in phenotype without a change in genotype — which in turn affects how cells read the genes. Epigenetic change is a regular and natural occurrence but can also be influenced by several factors including age, the environment/lifestyle, and disease state.

In a very simplified nutshell, environmental signals program our genes. We "turn on" or "turn off" genes according to how we live, think, act; basically, how we behave. So many people think they are destined for certain health conditions based on genetics and that there is nothing they can do to change that, but this is simply not true. Of course, if you believe it is true and you live in an environment that promotes it to be true, then you will likely be powerless against the "programming."

For example, my mom had a heart attack at a young age. Heart attacks run on her side of my family. I have a friend who is a cardiologist who urged me to come in to get preventive care for heart problems because of my family's medical history. So, I did. I agree it is something I should pay attention to. As a matter of fact, this knowledge can help me determine how to live. It can drive my behaviors, such as nutrition and exercise choices, sauna usage, sunlight exposure, supplements to take, stress reduction techniques to implement, and other types of preventive health care measures.

And because of doing all those things, my cardiac health profile is perfect. I have lived a different life, with a different perspective, eating different foods, moving my body differently, and in a different environment than my mother did. This has probably contributed to a changed personal health outcome.

Many people have been trained to believe that genes determine destiny. But what really happens is that we manifest these faulty beliefs. What if it's not our genes that determine our health outcomes but rather our thoughts and actions (often passed down through generations)?

If we can't grasp this way of approaching our life, we will feel like powerless victims, destined for certain health problems, financial issues, relationship problems—just because that is what has been programmed for us. But the truth is, you are NOT powerless. You have the power to change your thoughts and change the outcomes for your health and your life as a whole.

Something you may have heard about in the news is a good example of this. Ever heard of the BRAC-1 gene? It's the breast cancer gene. Actress Angelina Jolie went through a double mastectomy because she found out she had that gene. Here's the thing—even with that gene, you only have 50% chance of getting breast cancer. There is an alternative to a mastectomy.

I have absolutely no judgment for anyone's choices, but personally I would study those who have the gene and don't get cancer and do what they do. I would seriously consider implementing their habits into my lifestyle and monitor my breast health carefully moving forward.

If you believe the BRAC-1 gene (or any gene or diagnosis) is a death sentence, then that will impact your outcome. The genes should not dictate your life and future, but your thoughts do. You can actually change your body's chemistry based on the way you think and based on how you deal with stress.

I have a friend named Sasha who had brain cancer in her twenties. She is lucky to be alive today. We were talking several years ago and she was reflecting on how she had lived her life prior to receiving her cancer diagnosis. She had family members who had cancer and it terrified her. She would lie in bed at night saying, "I don't want cancer; please don't give me cancer." She allowed these thoughts and fears to overtake her mind. Then she was diagnosed with brain cancer. Her greatest fear came true.

She now realizes how her thoughts and focus could have contributed to her diagnosis and takes ownership of that. She is doing great today and learned how powerful one's mind can be. Focusing on fears and the worst-case scenario is not a healthy or fun way to live. It can breed problems and illness. Sasha now focuses on positivity, health, and healing. As a matter of fact, she has been in full remission for sixteen years and is just finishing nursing school. What a beautiful full-circle story!

We are driving the ship. There's resistance to believing this. We don't want to believe our thoughts can create or prevent disease. We like to be able to evade ownership. But until we take ownership, we will simply be victims.

One aspect of my career for decades was to help corporations support their employees, especially in learning to manage stress in healthy ways. We have performed substantial data analysis to find that most doctors' visits are a result of stress-related issues. Whether it's due to financial stress, relationship stress, or some other stressor, stress controls thoughts and lives, which manifests in disease and more stress. It's a terrible cycle that can send you into a downward spiral emotionally and health-wise.

We have to stop and ask: What are we attracting into our lives? The more we focus on these negative things, the more negativity we bring into our lives. This can have a major impact on health and well-being.

A study conducted at the University of San Francisco headed by Dr. Dean Ornish, a nutrition expert, and Dr. Peter Caroll, a noted urologist, and published in the *Journal of Urology* (September 2005) found that men with early-stage prostate cancer who make changes in diet and lifestyle may stop or reverse the progression of their illness.

Essentially, with stress reduction, meditation, and good nutrition, their health outcomes improved and without these practices, they declined. Seems pretty amazing and even outrageous, doesn't it? But the truth is, lifestyle controls genes, not the other way around.

Once we adopt this mindset, and start using our body as a tool to decipher our soul's deepest secrets in an effort to expose and correct them, we can experience fuller, healthier lives void of the fear and powerlessness that so many allow to overcome them.

By learning to listen to your body and responding with awareness, you take back the power that so many of us have been taught to hand over. This isn't just about healing physical discomfort; it's about reclaiming ownership of your health, your decisions, and your life. You don't have to wait for a diagnosis or breakdown to start paying attention. The moment you tune in and trust your body's wisdom, you become the authority, and that is one of the most powerful moves you can make.

To help you integrate this message and deepen your connection to your body as a source of power and guidance, journal your answers to the following questions:

- What signals has my body been sending me lately? Have I been ignoring or numbing any of them?
- When was a time I pushed through pain, fatigue, or discomfort? What was the deeper cost?

- What physical symptoms or patterns seem to repeat in my life? What might they be trying to tell me?
- Have I ever given away my authority when it came to my health? What would I do differently now?
- How would my life change if I trusted my body as a wise and intelligent messenger rather than something to manage or fix?
- What is one small practice I can begin today to reconnect with my body's guidance, without needing a crisis to wake me up?
- Are there any illnesses or diseases that run in my family that I feel powerless against? Might there be another factor contributing to the passing down of this health situation from generation to generation, other than genes?

CHAPTER 9

Reclaiming the Power of Your Body: Biology in Balance

Now that you understand how to listen to your body and how it receives instructions from your thoughts, beliefs, and emotional patterns, it's time to look at what you can do to help it thrive. If your body has been acting as a messenger, showing you where healing is needed, this next part of the journey is about reclaiming your role as its strongest ally.

There is no shortage of books or experts telling you to eat clean and exercise more, or providing ways to optimize your physical health for better results. (I am throwing no shade here, this includes me. My first book, *Back to Balance: Crack Your Mind, Body, Spirit Code to Transform Your Health*, has some focus on this.) Of course, these practices are important, but this chapter isn't about what you *do* to your body, but instead what you can help it remember. The body has innate power that already lives *within it*.

Your physical form is not just a reflection of your inner world; it is also a powerful vessel with its own wisdom, rhythm, and regenerative capabilities. Your body is not a machine to be fixed or upgraded. It is a brilliant, intuitive vessel designed to heal, protect, and thrive when aligned with its natural rhythms. Rather than prescribing rigid protocols or chasing peak performance, we will explore how to restore trust in your body's wisdom and its ability to regulate, regenerate, and respond when given precisely what it needs.

In order to shift from simply decoding your symptoms to actively stimulating your strength, you must learn to partner with your body's natural intelligence to build resilience, restore vitality, and reclaim your power on a physical level. The many ways you can achieve that naturally follow.

One of the most profound ways you can empower your body is utilizing the awesome power of the sun. Sunlight exposure, in proper amounts, is critical to a healthy body. Many people are light-deprived (spending too much time indoors), creating a kind of malnutrition that affects mood, immunity, and sleep. Couple that with constant stimulation from our electronic screens' blue light, which disrupts melatonin production and alters circadian signals, and you have an epidemic of physiological processes gone awry.

The sun is not just a source of light; it's a source of life. Every living being on this planet is wired to respond to the rhythms of sunlight. Exposure to natural light—especially in the morning—acts as a master regulator of our circadian rhythm, the internal clock that governs everything from sleep-wake cycles to hormone production and cellular repair. Morning sunlight signals the brain to release cortisol (in healthy amounts), boosting alertness and energy while setting the timer for evening melatonin release to support restful sleep.

Sunlight also delivers a full spectrum of wavelengths, each color vibrating at its own frequency, offering unique benefits. This spectrum of wavelengths is released into our atmosphere (and seen by the eye as various colors) in the order of a rainbow, then descends in the same manner. So, first thing in the morning, red light comes out. Then, orange is added, followed by yellow, green, blue, and purple. Then they reverse out in the opposite sequence. Purple leaves, blue leaves, green leaves, yellow leaves, orange leaves, and finally, red leaves at sunset. This is why sunrise and sunset have those beautiful hews of red; red is the longest wavelength and stays out all day. This would make purple/violet the shortest wavelength and the color that is out the shortest amount of time during the day. If you think about how we draw a rainbow, that makes sense: red is the longest, purple is the shortest, and the others fall in between.

For this reason, it is important and helpful to your body that you get outside every so often during the day. (I try for at least five minutes hourly.) You want to expose your skin and eyes to the increasing and decreasing wavelengths of light so your body can signal proper hormone production and keep the body attuned to the rhythm of nature, which changes with the seasons. Without these cues, our bodies are confused and shut down production of important hormones.

There is a lot of science around what each wavelength of light helps with, too much for us to explore in this book. But our bodies evolved under the sun, and we need every color of the rainbow to maintain proper health. Red and near-infrared light, for example, penetrate deeply into the body, stimulating mitochondrial function and promoting healing at the cellular level. These wavelengths can activate production of ATP, the energy currency of the cell, which fuels everything from muscle recovery to cognitive clarity.

Ultraviolet light, in the right doses, catalyzes the production of vitamin D, a hormone-like compound essential for immune regulation, bone strength, mood stability, and even reproductive health. Without enough sunlight, the body often struggles with sluggish hormone signaling, poor sleep, inflammation, and weakened immunity.

And it's not just biology—it's rhythm. Aligning with the sun's natural cycles helps recalibrate your entire being. When you wake with the sun, spend time in natural daylight, and dim your lights as the sun goes down, your body remembers its innate wisdom. Hormones fall back into balance. Mood stabilizes. Energy becomes more consistent. It's not just healing; it's a homecoming.

Here are some starter tips to help you introduce safe, consistent sun exposure and work with light to power your body:

- Download an app called Dminder (dminder.ontometrics.com) to track your safe sun allowance. This app bases your sun exposure on your skin type by using a Fitzpatrick skin type classification (based off a quiz you complete), which categorizes skin based on its response to UV light and its natural pigmentation. It then combines the time of day with your location to tell you exactly how much sun you can get to receive optimal vitamin D without burning (damaging) your skin. This app was a game changer for me! You will learn so much about your skin, the sun, and its intensity at any given time, and how much vitamin D your body makes naturally at different times of year. I highly recommend downloading and using this app!

- Ditch the sunglasses. Unless using them is a safety measure, such as avoiding glare while driving, they're blocking the important spectrum of light from your eyes. Your eyes seeing the colors of the sun, as they rise and set through the day, is super important for the health of your body. Even just taking them off five or ten minutes out of the hour is helpful.

- Get outside *immediately* in the morning. Even if you can only get outside for five minutes, do it. Even in the winter, even in the cold, bundle up and get that sunlight in your eyes (and when possible, on your skin). If you can see the sunrise, bonus points! This will help your body get into regulation in such a major way. The same is true for being outside at sunset, which is much easier for most people in our society. You do not need to see the actual sunrise or sunset. Just being outside at that time and exposing your eyes to the rays is key. If you cannot get outside, open a door or look out the window. It is better to look out a screen than through glass, but every step is better than no natural light exposure.

- Once the sun sets, you should do whatever you can to avoid blue light exposure, as well as full-spectrum light bulbs (think LED or bright white lights). This is tough in the average person's life.

There are a few ways to combat this. One is buying blue light blocking glasses and wearing them after sunset. There are many on the market, but the majority of them are not scientifically backed. There is one brand that is scientifically backed and well worth the extra spend: Swanwick (www.swanwicksleep.com). I have a few pairs and keep them in different areas of my home to make sure they're always available. You might find, like me, that after watching TV in the evening, you stay wired and awake, even though you are tired. But if you have your Swanwick glasses on (in bed, or simply leading up to bedtime), you will dose off within a few minutes. You can also download apps onto your computers and phones (or simply adjust the settings, if your devices have the ability) that take the blue light down and increase the amber or red light at sunset. There is an app called F.lux (justgetflux.com) that I use on my computer and it works wonderfully. It knows the exact time of sunset, so when my computer moves from blue to amber, I know it is time for my day to start winding down. You can also buy red or amber light bulbs to use in the areas of your home that you use most after sundown. This prevents the bright bulbs from stimulating your brain and body.

- Your body produces vitamin D when UVB (ultraviolet B) rays from the sun hit your skin. However, UVB rays don't reach the Earth's surface in certain areas during the winter months, especially when the sun is below a 30° angle in the sky. This happens in latitudes above 37° North or below 37° South (think: Detroit, Boston, Chicago, Denver, Northern California, Europe, Canada, etc.). Between approximately November and March, the sun stays too low in the sky in these locations for the skin to synthesize vitamin D, even on sunny days. So, while it is still important and necessary to go outside so your eyes and skin can be exposed to the spectrum of light, you will not make vitamin D. You must either supplement or use artificial light. I do both. I take a high-quality vitamin D supplement (with K2 for bone support), but I also use a light box called Sperti (www.sperti.com) in those months to combat the lack of sun over a 30° angle in the sky.

Discussion about sun exposure naturally leads into the importance of honoring sleep cycles and circadian rhythms. The body operates on a finely tuned internal clock, and light—especially natural sunlight—is its primary timekeeper. Disruptions in this rhythm affect not only sleep quality but hormone balance, energy, digestion, and even emotional regulation. The ideal solution would be to go to bed at sundown and wake up at sunrise. While that isn't always possible, simply trying your best to move closer to this will help. Reclaiming the body's power starts with syncing our lifestyle to nature's rhythms, not overriding them.

From this foundation, we can explore more advanced ways to support the body's innate intelligence. One of the most powerful yet overlooked concepts is metabolic flexibility—the body's ability to shift between fuel sources like glucose and fat depending on need. Tapping into states like ketosis can stimulate neurogenesis, mental clarity, and reduced inflammation. This ability to adapt is a marker of vitality, and learning how to engage it through diet and lifestyle can unlock remarkable healing potential. The metabolic state of ketosis is not the same as the "keto diet." Many try to use the keto diet to achieve the metabolic state of ketosis, but it is difficult to achieve by simply cutting carbohydrates out of one's diet. To achieve the metabolic state of ketosis, one must also reduce protein intake and increase fat intake significantly. There are three types of ketones that the body releases: acetoacetate, beta-hydroxybutyrate, and acetone. Acetoacetate is tested with urine strips and beta-hydroxybutyrate and acetone by blood or finger prick. Acetone can also be tested with breath testing meters. If these ketones aren't being released in the body, you are not in ketosis, no matter how strictly you are adhering to a keto diet. The release of these ketones are the indicators that an individual is in the metabolic state of ketosis, which means that the body is primarily using fat for energy, instead of carbohydrates. It is not easy to get into ketosis, but it is important to switch between metabolic states on occasion. This is called metabolic flexibility.

Related to ketosis is the process of autophagy, the body's built-in clean-up system, which becomes more active during fasting. Intermittent or prolonged fasts (done with proper medical direction) can clear out damaged cells and stimulate regeneration. These practices not only support longevity but also give the body time and space to heal from chronic inflammation, toxicity, and stress. It is important to be educated on fasting and understand the downfalls. Too much fasting can lower levels of leptin, an important hormone. If someone is thin and fasting too often, their leptin can drop below healthy levels. I had this happen to me and had to spend a couple years working on increasing my leptin. It wasn't easy to raise after I did the damage. However, this is rare, and the majority of people have a leptin level that is too high, thus pointing to the need for occasional or prolonged fasting. If in doubt, you can check your leptin levels with a simple blood test your physician can send you for.

Cold and heat therapies offer the body powerful tools for regeneration and resilience. While they may seem like opposites, both activate vital biological responses, especially through the production of shock proteins, which help the body repair and adapt under stress. Cold exposure, such as ice baths or cold showers, can reduce inflammation, enhance circulation, and stimulate the release of norepinephrine, a neurotransmitter linked to mood and focus. It also activates cold shock proteins, which protect neurons and promote neurogenesis. Women do not need the water to be as cold as men do to receive benefits. On the other side, heat therapy—from saunas to infrared treatments—trigger heat shock proteins, which help repair damaged proteins, support cellular detoxification, and increase stress tolerance. Alternating between heat and cold exposure can boost mitochondrial efficiency, improve cardiovascular health, and build mental toughness. These natural therapies remind us that the body thrives not through constant comfort but by learning to recover from purposeful, temporary, and intentional stressors. The key is in the dose—too much stress is damaging but just the right amount builds long-term vitality.

Hormonal balance is another pillar of physical empowerment. Our hormones regulate everything from energy and mood to fertility and metabolism, yet many modern lifestyle habits disrupt this delicate system. Chronic stress, environmental toxins, circadian disruption, natural light deprivation, and sleep deprivation all contribute to hormonal dysregulation. Supporting the endocrine system with restorative practices like rest, light exposure, nervous system regulation, and nutrient-dense nourishment helps restore hormonal harmony.

Just as we consider what enters the body, we must also support what exits the body. The lymphatic system, our body's detox highway, thrives with movement, hydration, and stimulation. Practices like dry brushing, rebounding, infrared sauna use, liver castor oil packs, and intentional sweating help flush out stagnation and encourage cellular renewal. These are not beauty rituals—they are biological necessities for vibrant health.

The gut-brain connection is another vital key. Our microbiome directly influences immune function, mental health, and emotional resilience. A healthy gut supported by fermented foods, prebiotics, and probiotics, and with limited exposure to gut-damaging chemicals, becomes the fertile ground for mental clarity and physical strength. It's not just about digestion—it's about whole-body integration.

Alongside this, mineral replenishment is essential. Many people unknowingly suffer from mineral depletion, which affects everything from muscle function to mood. Magnesium, sodium, potassium, and trace minerals are often stripped from modern water and processed food. Supporting the body with remineralized water, trace mineral drops, mineral based supplements, and mineral-rich foods brings back balance at a foundational level.

Another underappreciated factor in long-term vitality is bone mineral density. As we age, bone loss quietly robs us of strength, good posture, height, and resilience. Proactively supporting bone health through weight-bearing movement, proper nutrition, and hormonal support is a revolutionary act of care, especially for women. I was recently certified to teach a specialized yoga sequence designed to naturally support and improve bone mineral density. This method is backed by scientific research and has demonstrated measurable results in clinical trials. I now teach it online and am thrilled to report that many have already seen improvements in their bone mineral density through this simple, accessible practice. While conventional wisdom often suggests that pharmaceutical intervention is the only option, that's simply not true. Natural and proactive approaches can be highly effective, especially when started early. Maintaining strong bones is far easier than trying to rebuild density once it's been lost.

When we speak of empowerment, we must also include reproductive and sexual health. For women, this might mean learning to sync with menstrual cycles, seed cycling, or understand how their energetic patterns shift across the month. Cycle syncing is the practice of aligning diet, exercise, work, and self-care routines with the four phases of the menstrual cycle—menstrual, follicular, ovulatory, and luteal—to optimize energy, mood, and hormone balance. By honoring the body's natural rhythms, women can tap into the natural strengths of each phase of their menstrual cycle, leading to more balanced hormones, increased energy, improved mood, and greater productivity with less burnout. Seed cycling is a natural approach to supporting hormonal balance in women, particularly during the menstrual cycle. It involves consuming specific seeds during different phases of the cycle. For all people, sexual energy is a source of vitality, not something to suppress or misuse. Kabbalah and other ancient traditions have long honored the creative power of sexuality as life force. When honored consciously, it becomes a wellspring of strength.

We also nourish the body through the senses. The nervous system responds deeply to light, sound, smell, and texture. Reducing blue light, incorporating aromatherapy, choosing healing music or silence, and immersing in nature are not luxuries. They are inputs that shape how safe and supported the body feels. Sensory nourishment recalibrates the body on a subtle but powerful level.

From the ground up, we reclaim vitality through practices like earthing or grounding—walking barefoot on natural surfaces to help regulate the body's electrical charge, reduce inflammation, and improve sleep. It's a simple act with profound physiological effects. There are even earthing pads, mattresses, sheets, and blankets that you can use to sleep grounded all night. Similarly, posture and physical alignment play a huge role in energy flow, organ health, and even hormonal signaling. Corrective movement, chiropractic care, and mindful daily posture support the body's natural balance and prevent the long-term wear that leads to pain and depletion.

And of course, movement itself is essential—not as punishment or aesthetic pursuit, but as medicine. The right kind and amount of movement varies per person and season, but all bodies thrive with motion. Whether it's walking, dancing, strength training, yoga, or restorative stretching, movement activates the systems that keep us alive and awake.

Speaking of seasons, honoring the seasons means living in harmony with the natural rhythms that govern not only the earth but our own internal biology. Just as nature shifts through cycles of growth, rest, renewal, and harvest, our bodies are designed to move through similar patterns. In the colder, darker months, we're called to slow down. During this time, we favor warming, grounding foods like root vegetables, broths, and healthy fats; restorative movement like stretching, walking, or yin yoga; and longer, deeper sleep as the nights grow longer. In contrast, spring and summer invite lightness—fresh greens, seasonal fruits, more vigorous movement, and expanded social and creative energy. By listening to these cues and aligning our food, movement, rest, and even emotional expression with the seasons, we support our full body—our nervous system, metabolism, immunity, and overall vitality. This cyclical living reconnects us with ancient intelligence: the wisdom of being in sync with the earth itself.

To bring all of this full circle, we must remember that healing and empowerment don't come from controlling the body but from learning to honor it. One of the most intimate ways you can strengthen the mind-body connection is through ritual—not rigid routine, but intentional, reverent acts that affirm the body's healthy position. This might include body oiling, massage, slow movement, or bath rituals, simple practices that speak to the body in a language it understands: presence, respect, love. These rituals remind us that the body is not a problem to be solved, but a partner in our empowerment. When we treat it as such, it becomes a powerful ally in the life we are creating, an instrument of intuition, resilience, and grace.

CHAPTER 10

Reclaiming the Power of Your Mind: From Shadow to Strength

Now that we've explored ways to reclaim the power of your body, we will move on to ways you can reclaim the power of your mind. Most of us were never taught how powerful our minds are—or how dangerous they can become when left on autopilot. We live in a world that often encourages disconnection from ourselves: numbing pain, ignoring intuition, chasing external validation. And yet, the most radical transformation begins when you stop looking outside and start going within.

This chapter is about reclaiming your mental power by learning to witness, rewire, and integrate every part of you—especially the parts you've disowned. This is the path from shadow to strength.

There is no such thing as a purely negative experience. Every setback, every heartbreak, every shadowy corner of our psyche can become a source of strength if we're willing to face it. Many of the most painful moments in my life became portals to the most powerful. The shift happened not because the circumstances changed, but because I changed—starting with the way I thought.

The truth is, what we believe becomes our reality. Our thoughts are not random; they are the architects of our lives. If you constantly tell yourself life is hard, people can't be trusted, or success is reserved for the lucky, your brain will work overtime to prove you right. It will filter out opportunities that contradict your narrative. It will find evidence to support the struggle. If you decide life is working for you, your brain will find support for that too.

This is called confirmation bias—and it can either imprison you or set you free. Your mind favors information that aligns with what you already believe. This mechanism once helped us survive, but today it often keeps us trapped. What once kept us safe is now keeping us small.

And we all do it. We all carry around these inherited or accumulated narratives, many of which we didn't even choose, nor would we consciously. We absorbed them from parents, teachers, religion, society, or trauma. These thoughts become default settings. They whisper in our heads when we're tired, triggered, or uncertain: *You're not enough. You'll mess it up. It never works out for you.* And unless we become conscious of them, they run the show.

But thoughts are not truths. They are habits. And habits can be changed.

The stories you tell yourself are powerful. But they are also changeable. That's where your power begins.

To change your life, you must begin with the stories you tell yourself. Ask: *What stories am I rehearsing in my mind? Whose voice are they in? And do I even agree with them?*

When you see life as something that happens *to* you, you operate from victim consciousness. You react instead of respond. You feel helpless, bitter, stuck. I've been there. And I learned that the more I told myself I was powerless, the more powerless I became.

But once I recognized I could choose to view life as happening *for* me, I shifted into creator consciousness. I started to see challenges as lessons. I stopped repeating the story of pain and started writing a new one. Even my chronic illnesses, injuries, and burnout transformed into turning points when I changed the way I thought about them.

When we operate from a victim mindset, we hand over the pen and let life write our story. We feel helpless, reactive, and at the mercy of circumstances.

But the shift to creator consciousness is a shift into agency. It's not about pretending life is always easy. It's about choosing to respond from power instead of powerlessness. It's about seeing hardship as a setup

RECLAIMING THE POWER OF YOUR MIND: FROM SHADOW TO STRENGTH

for growth. You may not control what happens, but you *do* control what you make it mean.

When you shift from victim to creator, you stop asking, *Why is this happening to me?* and start asking, *What is this here to teach me?*

Your mind listens closely to the stories you repeat. And it responds by creating more of the same. If you say, "This is impossible," your brain shuts down options. If you say, "There must be another way," your brain starts looking for new ways. Rewiring starts with awareness, and a willingness to change the narrative.

A creator mindset allows you to make your own reality. Rather than letting life toss you around, you consciously, with power, create the life of your dreams. You see opportunities where others see nothing. You will turn tragedy into triumph, trauma into success. When you are in this mindset, you rule your life. Your brain is firing out powerful messages of certainty, possibility, and positivity. Your brain sees the best in everyone you meet, finds the good in every situation, and sends a constant flow of uplifting, inspiring thoughts that keep you happy, healthy, and energized.

Many people assume that mindset work is just a spiritual buzzword or a surface-level tactic. But when practiced deliberately, it becomes a lifestyle shift. This is not about pretending everything is great. It's about acknowledging the power you have to interpret, reframe, and redirect your energy, especially in hard moments. That is where real strength lives.

But there's a reason this kind of change is hard—it requires confronting the shadows.

Inside each of us are disowned parts, what Jungian psychology calls the "shadow." These are the traits we've been shamed for, rejected for, or punished for having. Maybe you learned to hide your anger, ambition, sensuality, or sensitivity to feel safe or accepted.

We've been taught to hide, deny, or suppress certain traits, thus creating our shadows.

But what you disown doesn't disappear. It operates in the

background, draining your energy and influencing your decisions from the shadows. It shows up in our reactivity. In our resistance. In our defensiveness, judgment, control, perfectionism, or fear. Shadows are not bad. They're wounded parts of ourselves. And they hold incredible power—if you're willing to turn toward them instead of away from them.

When we deny our anger, it leaks out in sarcasm or self-sabotage. When we repress our sensitivity, we become emotionally detached or over-controlled. When we bury our desire, we numb ourselves with food, work, or endless scrolling. The cost of shadow denial is exhaustion and disconnection.

Reclaiming your power means reclaiming all of you. Even the parts that feel messy or hard to love. Especially those parts.

When you meet your shadow with curiosity instead of judgment, you begin to integrate it. You stop fighting against yourself and start reclaiming the strength hidden in the traits you once thought made you "too much."

Anger becomes boundary setting. Sensitivity becomes intuition. Ambition becomes leadership.

Ask yourself: what parts of me have I tried to hide or reject? Where do I feel triggered, and why? What am I afraid people might see?

The more you integrate your shadow, the more you own all parts of yourself, the less energy you spend fighting yourself. And that energy becomes available for healing, creativity, and deep inner power.

This is the essence of self-empowerment. You don't need to be fixed. You need to be reclaimed.

So how do you begin?

Shadow work, or shadow dialoguing, is all about finding these parts of yourself that you hide or deny and unifying them with your conscious self. Unifying the two allows you to become a whole being.

Shadow dialogue challenges you to choose a part of yourself that you suppress and ask it questions. Examples of the shadow selves you may deny are:

- Jealous self
- Angry self
- Avoidant self
- Lazy self
- Controlling self
- Rebel self
- Martyr self
- Know-it-all self
- Victim self

Are you unaware of your shadow parts? If none on the above list speak to you, try the following visualization. Instead of trying to remember it, voice record yourself reading it and listen back while your eyes are closed.

Shadow Identification Visualization

- Imagine yourself waiting alone for a school bus to pick you up on the side of a long dirt road. You patiently wait because you're enjoying your time. The weather is perfect, you can hear the sound of birds, the sun is shining down on you with the perfect intensity.
- You see the bus far away, heading toward you. You are feeling excited as the bus approaches. You know your friends are on the bus and you are going somewhere exciting today, with everyone you enjoy spending time with. As the bus pulls up and opens its doors, you get increasingly excited.
- You board the bus. You see the bus is full and you're the last pick-up; everyone is already here! You walk to your seat and sit down.
- You look around the bus and you notice that each person on the bus is you, one of your sub-personalities, all different ages and with the various parts of your personality.
- You start to label each person. Maybe there is a studious you in the back; a protector or warrior you in the front. You see

a comedian you, making everyone laugh. The provider you is handing out party favors. The artist you is drawing everyone's picture. The empowered leader you is explaining the plan to everyone for today's activities. All the "yous" are there, doing whatever you do in that role.

- Everyone is having a great time! You arrive at your destination and the entire bus empties. You are last off.
- You get the feeling that someone was left behind. You know you were last off, but you are certain, so you go back on the bus.
- It looks empty, but you hear something from the back, so you walk toward the back of the bus.
- Once you are in the last row, you see someone hiding behind the seat. You can't tell who it is because they are hiding their face.
- You kindly invite this person to show him/herself. You reassure him/her that you are safe and wait patiently for him/her to show him/herself.

This is a wonderful visualization to help your shadow self emerge. You may find that more than one shadow emerges.

It is possible (and likely) that you have multiple shadows. For the next exercise, work with one shadow at a time.

- Sit or lie comfortably. Close your eyes and start by breathing deeply to relax yourself.
- Picture your shadow—the part of you you've tried to deny. Visualize it sitting beside you (or on the bus, if you're still working on the visualization from above).
- Be friendly and kind to your shadow self. Speak to it with compassion.
- Notice if she/he is insecure, scared, lonely.
- Tell your shadow self that it is safe to be here. Let it become an ally.
- Ask questions to this part of you:

- When did you come into existence?
- What are you afraid of?
- What do you need to feel safe?
- What do you want from me? From life? From others?
- What else do you have to say?
- Any other intuitive questions that arise inside of you.

Write or draw the answers, openly, without judgment. Let this part of you speak freely, telling you why it was created and what purpose it serves.

Your shadow parts create negative or limiting beliefs within you as a defense mechanism, to keep you safe. Once you start working on exposing your shadow selves, you will start to see the negative and limited beliefs. You can then correlate which beliefs were created by which shadows.

It's not enough to identify limiting beliefs—you must also interrupt them and replace them. This is the power of neuroplasticity: the ability of your brain to rewire itself based on new input.

Here are a few science-backed practices that will help:

1. Pattern Interruption

When you catch yourself spiraling into negative thought patterns (judgment, criticism, fear), pause. Take a deep breath. Instead of judging it, question it.

Ask yourself:

- Is this belief absolutely true?
- Who taught me this?
- What might be possible if I believed something different?

Then, interrupt the pattern. This can simply be by saying: This is not my truth anymore.

2. "In the Past...But Now" Practice

Sometimes I have a difficult time letting go of beliefs that I think are true in my life. It can feel like I am gaslighting myself when I repeat "mantras" and positive statements that don't line up with my lived experiences. It can feel like I am lying to myself or denying my reality.

A technique I use when this feeling is persistent is saying:

In the past, I believed [insert limiting belief]. But now and in the future, I choose to believe [insert empowering belief].

This works for me because I feel like it honors my current belief (or what is true in my life) by first stating "In the past, I believed..." But then it lets me move forward with what I want to create in the future by following up with "But now and in the future, I choose to believe..."

I couple this statement with arm gestures to cement the idea in my brain and body. I use my hand and pretend I am throwing something over my shoulder and behind me when I speak of the past limiting belief. (I am literally putting the past limiting belief behind me.) Then I open my arms wide in front of me, embracing future possibilities, when speaking of future beliefs. Sometimes I do this physically and other times I simply mentally envision the motions.

Examples:

In the past, I believed success was hard to achieve. But now and in the future, I choose to believe success flows to me with ease.

In the past, I believed I had to struggle to be worthy. But now and in the future, I know I am worthy just by being me.

It is helpful to identify your negative beliefs, then create and memorize these statements as a new mantra around the topic. Anytime you catch yourself with that negative belief, you can then interrupt the pattern and repeat your new mantra.

Repeat them aloud when you're alone and silently when you're with others. Make them part of your new operating system. The more you practice this, the more natural it becomes. This isn't about ignoring reality. It's about retraining your brain to expect something better.

3. Reframe the Story

Look at your situation with fresh eyes. Think of your situation as it stands today and consider how you would find a happy ending to this situation if you were writing a book.

Consider the following questions or prompts, then journal your happy ending:

- What else might be true?
- How could this be working for me?
- What is the gift in this situation?
- Show me how it gets better.
- How can I look at this situation differently?
- What opportunities are in this situation?
- How can I change myself from a victim to a victor?

4. Visualization

Imagine your life going right. Picture yourself already embodying the confidence, peace, and wholeness you desire. Your brain will begin wiring toward that vision.

Science supports what spirituality has long known: your thoughts create your experience. Your brain doesn't know the difference between a vividly imagined scenario and a real one. That's why visualization is such a powerful tool.

When you visualize a positive outcome, you create a new memory in your brain—a memory that makes it more likely for that experience to occur. Pair that with a practice like gratitude, and you start reshaping your entire mental landscape.

Gratitude is more than a feel-good exercise. It rewires the brain toward optimism and expands your awareness of possibility. According to author Shawn Achor, he has scientific research showing that participants increased happiness and decreased depressive symptoms after twenty-one days of completing only one of the following two-minute exercises.

The powerful (two-minute) daily practices from Shawn Achor's *Happiness Advantage* research:

- **Gratitude Practice** – Write three new things you're grateful for each day. Be specific.
- **The Doubler** – Reflect on one positive experience from the day and describe it in detail. Reliving the experience "doubles" the positive effect in your life.
- **Meditation** – Just two minutes a day of meditation shows positive effects.
- **Fun Fifteen** – (This is the only habit that takes more than two minutes.) Fifteen minutes of fun, active cardio exercise proved equivalent to taking an anti-depressant for six months.
- **Conscious Acts of Kindness** – Send one sincere message of appreciation to someone in your life each day. This should be a different person each day. This is the most powerful habit of the five.

Most of us need to consciously create happiness to combat something psychologists call negativity bias. Negativity bias is when the brain specifically remembers negative things to keep us safe. Our brains were wired to notice and remember risky or dangerous situations so we could more easily respond to them.

Think of times when predators roamed the earth freely and how this helped us stay safe. While we typically don't have predators threatening us anymore, negative comments or situations can feel like a threat to us in today's world. These negative comments or situations can rule or control our brain in the same way a tiger did in the past.

Think about a typical day in your life. You may have received five praises or nice comments that day from your kids, coworkers, spouse, or other family and friends. Then one person said something cutting, sarcastic, or unkind. At the end of the day, what do you remember? The negative comment, right?

Bestselling author and expert on happiness Marci Shimoff offers tools to help us overcome our negativity bias:

- **Lookout for the Good** – As mentioned above, it is easy to focus on the one negative and miss the five positives. Be conscious about looking for the positive moments, the encouraging comments, the kindness surrounding you.
- **Savor It** – It takes twenty seconds for a neuro pathway to be solidified in the brain, so when positive events occur, you need to really savor them. Take at least twenty seconds to deeply feel and absorb any positive moment. Take the moment in with every sense you have.
- **Balance the Negative with the 3-to-1 Rule** – When you find yourself having a negative thought, intentionally look for three positive things to switch your thinking. This will help you create new habits that are more positive.

These aren't just habits. They're energetic shifts that change the way your brain, body, and spirit function.

Let's anchor this chapter in practices that will help you rewire your brain.

Reflection Practices

Journal Prompts:

- What repetitive thoughts have been holding me back?
- Where in my life am I playing small or blaming others?
- What parts of myself do I try to hide or suppress?
- When do I feel most empowered, and what thoughts precede that feeling?
- What beliefs have shaped my life up until now? Who gave me those beliefs? Do I want to keep them?

Daily Rewiring Practice:

- Notice when you criticize, complain, or judge.
- Interrupt the pattern. Say: "In the past, I believed… but now I choose to believe…"
- Repeat it out loud.
- Anchor it with a physical gesture (like throwing it behind you or opening your arms).

Visualization Exercise:

- Close your eyes.
- Imagine the most empowered version of yourself.
- What are they doing, saying, creating, radiating?
- Step into that energy.

Meditation Practice:

- Repeat the affirmation: I reclaim all parts of me. I am whole. I am worthy. I am powerful.

Gratitude Exercise:

- End each day with: "Today I'm grateful for…"
- Add one conscious act of kindness to close the loop.

RECLAIMING THE POWER OF YOUR MIND: FROM SHADOW TO STRENGTH

The shadow is not your enemy. It's your teacher. When you learn to sit with discomfort without running or numbing, you begin to integrate your wholeness. You are not your thoughts; you are the thinker, and you have the power to choose new ones. Empowerment means making peace with your humanity and choosing self-compassion instead of self-sabotage, alignment instead of perfectionism.

You'll never eliminate all the "negative" thoughts—and you shouldn't try to. But you can stop being ruled by them. You can stop believing them without question. And you can certainly stop letting them keep you from your purpose. This isn't about toxic positivity. It's about radical responsibility. And it's a lifelong practice. But with each conscious thought, each gentle reframe, each moment of self-awareness, you are building a life that reflects your true power.

This is what it means to take your power back—not with force, but with fierce compassion and conscious choice. Your mind is not the enemy. It's the gateway to the life you're here to create.

Let it be a powerful one.

CONCLUSION

Owning Your Power and Purpose

Research in psychology, sociology, and trauma recovery shows that while no family is perfect, certain core traits and dynamics in a family system dramatically increase the chances that a child grows into a resilient, emotionally intelligent, and empowered adult capable of success in all areas of life.

Key family traits that empower individuals include:

- Psychological safety – children are allowed to express thoughts, questions, and emotions without fear of ridicule or punishment. Mistakes are treated as learning opportunities. Children are not shamed for their emotions. Conflict is discussed without yelling or silence as a weapon.
- Open communication – emotions, boundaries, needs, and concerns can be talked about freely. Parents model vulnerability and repair ("I'm sorry. I was wrong. Let's talk about it."). Children are encouraged to articulate needs and practice empathy.
- Encouragement of autonomy – kids are allowed to make age-appropriate choices and explore their identify safely. They are encouraged to follow curiosity, solve problems, and speak up. Individuality is celebrated, not squashed.
- Boundaries and structure with flexibility – clear rules and expectations exist, but without rigidity or emotional withdrawal. Consequences are fair and explained. They match the action. Parents maintain the role of guides, not controllers.
- Unconditional love and secure attachment – love is not tied to

performance, achievements, or perfection. Parents are consistently emotionally present and attuned. Children know they are loved even when they make a mistake.
- Modeling of emotional regulation – adults regulate their emotions in healthy ways and take responsibility for them through apologies and self-reflection. Parents do not project their pain onto their children. Anger, sadness, and joy are all modeled without shame.
- Growth mindset culture – families talk about goals, learning, and progress instead of focusing on "success and failure." Challenges are framed as growth opportunities. Encouragement is promoted over criticism.
- Empowered conversations around finances – money isn't a taboo topic. Finances are taught, discussed, and modeled with transparency. Children learn about budgeting, investing, value creation, and tithing or philanthropy. Parents discuss money without stress or secrecy.
- Respect for the body and health – food, movement, rest, and emotions are connected and respected above all else. There is no body shaming, no food shaming, and parents model self-care without guilt.
- Spiritual framework – children are taught a sense of meaning, connection, and purpose while being encouraged to explore spirituality, religions, and nature-based, ethical, or value-driven philosophies freely. Parents encourage internal reflection, wonder, admiration, and personal responsibility.

As you read that list, you likely noticed traits from your childhood or family that were both present and missing. The missing pieces are likely areas you are now working on, to improve yourself. We all have an opportunity to parent ourselves later in life and complete the puzzle of our upbringing.

This book was written to help you do just that: take ownership of the deficits in your life and turn them into your biggest power center through transformation.

We all experience varying levels of trauma, both from our upbringing and many from traumatic events later in life. You've likely heard of PTSD (Post Traumatic Stress Disorder), which can follow accidents, injuries, combat exposure, assault, natural disasters, etc. with various symptoms like flashbacks, nightmares, intrusive thoughts about the trauma, negative changes in mood, heightened anxiety or irritability, and difficulty sleeping.

But there is also something called Post Traumatic Growth (PTG), which is a lesser-known cousin of PTSD, discovered in the 1990s by psychologists Richard Tedeschi and Lawrence Calhoun. Based on their research, they described five categories of growth that can occur over time after trauma:

1. Survivors of trauma recognize and embrace new opportunities.
2. They forge stronger relationships with loved ones as well as with other victims who suffered in a similar way.
3. They cultivate inner strength through the knowledge that they have overcome tremendous hardship.
4. They gain a deeper appreciation for life.
5. Their relationship to religion or spirituality changes and evolves.

You can find more information at this article from *Psychology Today*, (www.psychologytoday.com/us/basics/post-traumatic-growth), or in Tedeschi and Calhoun's 1998 book on the subject, *Posttraumatic Growth: Positive Changes in the Aftermath of Crisis (Personality and Clinical Psychology)*.

I like to think about PTSD being more of a nervous system response, while PTG is the result of longer-term healing and processing of trauma. The personal strength, new perspectives, improved relationships, and spiritual growth that occur from PTG are influenced by:

- Your social support
- Your coping strategies
- Your personal traits like optimism and openness to change

These are the key factors in transforming your trauma into triumph.

Do you have adequate social support? Review the family traits above and consider the people in your life. These are things we want not only in the family we were born into, but the family we choose later in life.

Do you have coping strategies that will lead you down the right path? Much of this book was devoted to developing them, but there is always more work that can be done.

Have you developed personal traits like optimism and openness to change? Again, this book was designed to take you down that path, but if you simply read the pages instead of working through the exercises, journaling, meditations, and other suggestions, it could have been intellectualized instead of internalized.

This process is true if you are recovering from trauma or simply trying to better your life. You don't need to identify with being a survivor of trauma to make changes to better your life.

Maybe you just keep facing challenges or frustrations in your life. The Kabbalists teach—and I believe strongly—**that you have specific challenges come to you as a spiritual lesson for growth**. Every challenge has a gift on the other side of it. The trick is navigating the challenge to see the proper spiritual teaching. Once you find it, the challenge will fall away, instantly.

We have discussed so many ways to do this in the book, but quite often our ego is powerful at hiding the truth from us or stopping us from making true change. True change threatens the ego.

Sometimes finding a spiritual mentor or someone who can help you unlock the code is time and money well spent. This doesn't have to be a one-on-one relationship, although those are wonderful and empowering. Simply taking classes, online or in person, that can help you walk the process with a group of like-minded people is a powerful way to start. Not to mention, it also helps you build a community of supportive, new friends.

The Kabbalah Centre (www.kabbalah.com) is a great non-profit organization if you are looking for a next step. There are numerous other organizations and teachers out there as well.

My goal is to help you integrate this new connectedness in all aspects of your life. It's important to understand that you must maintain a certain level of balance and keep your mind-body-spirit healthy to stay connected. This will look different for everyone. It's about caring for your body and mind and feeding your soul in all the ways we have already discussed and however is appropriate for you, at any given time.

Keeping yourself in balance will empower you. You will no longer make decisions based on fear. In a balanced state, you can make decisions based on your intuition. The more you utilize your intuition, the more confidence you will have in it.

When I broke my leg and they told me it wasn't broken, I knew something was wrong—I had a nagging feeling. If I had listened to my instincts sooner, I would have saved myself a lot of pain. Today, that wouldn't happen because I know how to listen to and, most importantly, trust my intuition.

You will be able to keep practicing using your intuition for little life decisions and big ones. Once this becomes second nature, you will be in the universal flow—what I call "the sweet spot"! This is like a river of intuition; it becomes effortless. The right doors open, the wrong doors close. You are attuned and know which way to go. Being in the flow is a wonderful experience. You may not always know where the flow will take you, but you can trust the ride and know it will all make sense later as you begin to see the right pieces falling into place simply because you trusted yourself.

A major part of maintaining the balance you need to stay connected is knowing when to take a break. These days, I take a break when my body and intuition tell me, even when it doesn't really make sense. I take regular retreats to get back in balance—sometimes the retreats last a weekend, other times they are extended. Maybe you can't do that because you have family or financial obligations, but you can always find ways to retreat on a walk or by taking an internet/media fast or by cancelling all your plans for the weekend and resting.

What about taking your newfound confidence into the world around you? How will this impact others? As humans, we tend to think about ourselves independently. The truth is we are part of humanity. When you achieve a certain level of balance and begin listening to your intuition, you will likely find yourself thinking more globally than individually. There is a shift in perspective that only comes when you are in the right place of balance. You will find that the right thing to do isn't just what makes sense to you personally but what makes sense for the world around you.

You will begin thinking of others and be compelled to make decisions that will contribute to the greater good. When you are truly connected, your connection goes from self to the world as a whole. When the whole is doing better, you are personally doing better. Decisions might not make sense the way that they used to, but if you are listening to your intuition, you can trust you are doing the right thing.

Consider when a flock of birds is flying in the sky, forming the V. They are just effortlessly working as a team, unified. A lot of humans don't have that because they are ego-based. But when you are heart-based with others who are heart-based, unity happens. You are on the same plane and synergy happens naturally. Your intuition will bring you into line with others. One day, you'll look around and realize you are in the middle of a V formation.

If you do not follow your intuition, you will be essentially lying to yourself and, thus, weakening yourself. Also, it's safe to say that if you cannot trust yourself, you will have trust issues with others in your life. How can you trust someone else if you can't trust yourself? It all begins with connectedness and trust in self—and grows from that foundation.

As you take this new connectedness into the world, you may find you no longer need the approval of others. The more centered you become, the more you trust your instincts and the less you require another person's stamp of approval on your choices. Former people-pleasers will especially be amazed by the transformation that can take place once you step into your power.

Start small. Build the intuition muscle. Then you can confidently move to bigger decisions. Sometimes you will miss the mark and that's okay. Learn from it and try again. You will build and grow in your strength as you go. Practicing will increase confidence.

As you follow your intuition, keep in mind that your new life may not appeal to some of the people around you. Perhaps they were used to the old you and are slightly turned off by this stronger, more confident version. In my life, I have personally found my decisions do not always make me the most popular person. Here's the thing—if you are interested in being the most popular person, this may not be the right journey for you. But if you want the best life possible, then this is absolutely the way to go, so step into your power with confidence.

Once you have done the work to leave that place where your ego reigned and start to live in a heart-based/mind-based space, you will find you don't need to justify your behaviors anymore. Instead, you can trust you are doing the right thing for yourself, your family, and your world.

Taking back ownership of your life is the underlying theme of this book. By now, you should fully understand and accept that you have the power to change your life. Once you take ownership of your life and realize everything you are doing is manifesting in your life, you are in a position to make the necessary changes.

I want you to see your life, your trauma, and difficult moments as transformative tools for healing and drawing your most powerful gifts from the universe. The closer you get to the source of your problems, the closer you will find yourself to the gifts that are waiting for you on the other side of your pain.

Your purpose is not handed to you on a silver platter; it is found in the dark places you try to avoid. These dark places offer you power, not helplessness, and the only way to find your potential is to search for and light up those areas.

Imagine what might happen in the world if every single person took ownership of "their stuff" and what they are putting out into the universe. What if every person did the work to find peace internally? Amazing change would take place—it would be a global awakening. Each human being is either bringing others up or pulling them down by what they contribute to the universal field.

Now that you have this connection and have a way to tap into it, you can profoundly change your life and the lives of others, but you must be willing to take action and move forward with your new knowledge. How do you change your life and other people's lives with it? Do the work required to stay connected, grounded, and balanced, and simply trust yourself. This is what self-empowerment is all about.

I have full faith in you and total certainty of your success.

ABOUT THE AUTHOR

Cassie Sobelton is a health and wellness expert, bestselling author, and entrepreneur with a no-fluff approach to healing and empowerment. As the founder and CEO of Wellness Collection®, she delivers high-integrity supplements and holistic tools that support mind-body-spirit wellness.

A passionate advocate for emotional resilience, Cassie helps people break free from burnout, people-pleasing, and performative living to reclaim their power—calmly and clearly. Her work blends lived experience with grounded tools that empower readers to create boundaries, trust their intuition, and live boldly without compromising heartfelt empathy and compassion.

When she's not writing or running her company, Cassie enjoys quiet nature walks, mindful moments, and helping others return to the truth of who they really are.

CONNECT WITH ME

If *The Power Reset* spoke to something real in you, I'd love to stay in touch!

Visit CassieSobelton.com for free tools, guided practices, and deeper resources to help you apply what you've learned. Whether you're navigating burnout, setting boundaries, or simply craving more clarity in a distracted world, you'll find support that meets you where you are.

You can also join my email circle for practical insights, honest encouragement, and reminders to reconnect with yourself, especially when life feels full.

Prefer social? I share reflections and real-life tools on most major platforms @cassiesobelton.

You don't need to do it all. You just need space to hear yourself again. Let's keep going, together.

Made in United States
Cleveland, OH
23 October 2025

24530864R00066